THE BEST OF GRANTA
1889—1966

THE BEST OF
Granta

1889 — 1966

Edited by
JIM PHILIP
JOHN SIMPSON
NICHOLAS SNOWMAN

LONDON
SECKER & WARBURG

First published in England 1967 by
Martin Secker & Warburg Limited
14 Carlisle Street London W1

Printed in England by
Billing & Sons Limited
Guildford and London

Foreword

Everyone, except of course the actual editors, appears to have some definite concept of *Granta*'s function. To some it once existed as 'A College Joke To Cure The Dumps'; to those of a later generation, it became less amusing, more earnest. *Granta* through its years reflects very well the changes not only in Cambridge and its undergraduates but in the nation generally. These changes are discussed more fully in the introductory notes at the beginning of the two parts into which this anthology has been divided.

The one thing that must not alter, however, is that despite a shortage of good material as well as of money, editing *Granta* should be entertaining. The present editors have been attacked by undergraduates and dons alike both in and out of print— on one occasion they were threatened with a Luger which later proved to be of plastic. And there is, of course, always the embarrassment of poems about sailors and prostitutes by freshmen—strangers to the brothel as to any other port of call.

But change is evidently a very slow business. In 1924, writing in *The Granta and its Contributors, 1889–1914*, F. A. Rice sensed an apocalyptic future for the magazine:

'The paper now is properly organised. The editor has an Office to sit in, and, like the Psalmist, a Staff to comfort him. Perhaps I am over-bold when I write "properly organised". I dare say that thirty years ago they thought they were "properly organised", though we, today, wonder how they managed to go on with the business at all.

'One forgets that in 1950 people may be saying the same about us. They will smile gently, those successors of ours, when they turn up the volumes of the 'twenties. "Only twenty pages a week", they will say. "And look, they still used that old half-tone method for reproducing photographs. Why, even the cover isn't in more than two colours. An office—there couldn't have been much of an office in King Street, just a little room, perhaps. And how absurd—they only had a telephone in the 'twenties. It really makes one wonder how the paper has lasted. . . ." '

Granta's office today is an in-tray in a Silver Street bookshop, an application for a telephone was turned down, and, though we are more concerned with layout than were the 'twenties, colour is still an unrealised possibility.

But in the end individual editors and issues are transitory, and *Granta*'s lasting asset is its ability to survive. This anthology, we hope, demonstrates a little how *Granta*—that amorphous, ever-changing, longsuffering name—has yet retained something of a distinctive personality.

It is not always pleasant to see the work of one's youth brought out of the cupboard, and the editors and publishers wish to thank the contributors to this volume for submitting without payment to a possibly painful experience. Royalties earned from sales of the book are being paid into *Granta*'s bank account to help keep the magazine on its feet.

J. P.

J. S.

N. S.

Contents

8　　　　　　　　　　*Contents*

Contents 9

PART TWO: 1945–1966

The drawings on pages 156 and 192 are by Mark Boxer, and those on pages 199 and 222 by Oliver Hawkins.

Part One

1889—1939

Editors' Note

In anthologising *The Granta* from its inception in 1889 to its abrupt end with the outbreak of the Second World War, we have tried to bear in mind the extent to which it reflected changes in fashion and thought during that period. Perhaps our introduction to the first section of this book can do no better than point out briefly the patterns of change.

The period 1889–1939 falls easily into three eras: the first ends with the First World War, the second begins in 1919 and ends about 1933, and the third continues until the outbreak of war. Realising that it would be all too easy to drop into a slipshod discussion of themes, we have tried to tie ourselves down to describing and analysing three separate issues of *The Granta*, all of which were printed at the start of their respective periods.

The Granta of Friday 18 October 1889 opens with a mock-solemn address to freshmen (editorials at this time tended to centre around the institutional features of university). The tone is bantering, a little heavy, perhaps self-conscious:

'A modest demeanour suits better with a smooth face than a defiant swagger which is supposed by a few to be the highest attribute of man. Of cigars, etc., we may say that even the cheapest and smallest have been known, at first, to produce an amount of discomfort quite out of

proportion to their price and size. Nor can a profound
judgment in clarets and champagnes be inferred from a
considerable acquaintance with the light ale which is, we
believe, the ordinary beverage of a schoolboy.'

The paraphernalia of the gentleman—the cigars, the claret
—reveal not simply the writer's background, but also posit an
entire society which would accept such things as the normal
accoutrements of the good life.

Following the editorial come five sub-Miltonic stanzas and
eight pages of the feature 'Motley Notes', a blend in the all-
round tradition of social, sporting and Union smalltalk:

'Muttlebury and Gardner won a magnificent race for
the Goblets by the skin of their teeth . . .'

How limited, and yet how accomplished the nature of the
classics-based education of the time could be is clear from the
rambling couplets congratulating the Master of Trinity on the
birth of a son, which follow. The tone resembles *Punch*—as
much the lodestar for *Granta* men in the 'nineties as the
Thomson Organisation is today—the manner echoes the Savoy
Operas, and the matter is the parings of a classical upbringing:

'A Gradus ad Parnassum, full of epithet and synonym,
A Corpus Poetarum, such as classics love to edit, he
Will furnish, let us hope, a bright example of heredity.'

The ties with the public school are close; the last item in the
issue—'Compulsory Games at Public Schools'—shows this:

'So long as most English boys are vigorous and healthy,
most of them will delight in the physical exercise that
cricket, rowing and football provide.'

Thirty-three years later *The Granta* has not apparently developed very much. If there is a perceptible change in humour this seems to be because *Punch* has altered. In the issue of Friday 10 November 1922 a cartoon catches exactly the tone of *Punch*. One tramp is talking to another outside a pub:

'Says he can stand any number of drinks, and blimey, we goes inside and he never stands me one.'

The form of the magazine has changed scarcely at all; what has changed, presumably as a result of the Great War, is the range of interests. In the cartoon quoted above there is at last a realisation that a class not wholly composed of bedmakers exists beyond the gates of the public school; 'Harvard Notes' have taken the place of 'Oxford Notes', and the Continent appears more frequently.

After an editorial concerned with the forthcoming election, and an article about travel abroad, things quickly settle down to what was for fifty years the main staple of *The Granta*'s diet—news items and genial amusement at the expense of landladies and Proctors:

'I dreamt I saw a Proctor "escalating",
Rushing up a quickly moving stair,
Followed by his bulldogs palpitating,
All his actions emulating,
Faithful and devoted little pair.'

The series 'Those in Authority' and the sports reports continue, but reviews of the arts assume an increasingly important place in the magazine. Cars and girls begin to figure prominently; the winning photo in *The Granta* Holiday Snapshot Competition shows a couple kissing on a beach.

Fourteen years later the issue of Wednesday 18 November 1936 demonstrates a more complete change than has apparently occurred before. Politics is now a main concern, and

humour, formerly *The Granta*'s raison d'être, is employed
rather more as a means of articulating this new interest. The
editorial, entitled 'Student Songs', reflects an uneasy awareness
of current events in Germany.

The Diary of the Week's Events satirises Nazi pomposity:

'ART FOR ARTSSAKE

(Englisch slogan from the Dekadenz). Twofold programme. Villagewooing by Bernard Shaw (compare
Goering) and great Insektplay of Kapek brother and
brother. Symbolismus by the Brightoner Repertory
Corps. The beforetime in Cambridge on various occasions
by Londoner critics outsingled Marne Maitland takes
thereat part.'

This last paragraph shows in its own way the increasing
importance of the arts for *The Granta*. The pages devoted to
the theatre, art, films, records, and above all books, now form
a major part of the magazine. The book reviews are serious;
in this issue books by Dos Passos, Santayana, W. J. Turner,
William Saroyan, Arthur Bryant, Louis Macneice and W. H.
Auden are discussed. Film reviews tend to be caustic—'they
certainly forgot to hire a cameraman . . .'—and comprehen-
sive. Jazz features regularly in the record reviews: 'Red Norvo
and his wife Mildred Bailey are probably equally famous in
their own spheres'.

This is the general picture of *The Granta*'s development, but
it does not do justice to the more impressive contributions
which have appeared over the years we have covered; the
following pages will show, we hope, what *The Granta* (as it
was called throughout the period in question) could achieve
at its best.

The Birth of The Granta

R. C. LEHMANN

January 18th 1889 should be a red-letter day in the history of Cambridge University, for it was on that date that *The Granta*, like a new planet, swam into our ken. I have been asked to tell the story of how this paper was founded. To do so I must go a few months further back.

There was at that time resident at Cambridge Mr Oscar Browning, a don whose pleasure it was to help many generations of Cambridge men. Wherever there was a club or an association that required a treasurer to keep its accounts in order Mr Browning occupied that place and did yeoman's service in it. He is now reporting us and our cause aright in Italy. At the same time there was resident at Trinity Hall an undergraduate named Guthrie who had a strong inclination to journalism of the lighter kind; thus he was led to publish a journal called *The Gadfly*. The connection between *The Gadfly* and *The Granta* does not immediately strike the mind, but wait a bit and you shall see how all things worked together for the establishment of *The Granta* by means of *The Gadfly*. *The Gadfly* issued only one number which contained almost as a matter of common form an interview with Mr Browning, but this interview was written with so much *verve* that Mr Browning not unnaturally took offence and appealed to the authorities to help him by preventing *The Gadfly* from being anything more than a single-number paper. To be brief, *The Gadfly* was suppressed, and Mr Guthrie saw his scheme for the establishment of an undergraduate paper dissolved into thin air. He decided to seek revenge.

It happened just then to be Mr Browning's intention to publish a journal mainly devoted to matters of educational interest; this was to be called *The Granta*. So Mr Guthrie arranged to produce a *Granta* of his own before Mr Browning was ready with his educational paper. He selected a cover and took Mr Lionel Holland and myself into his counsels. He also decided, in order to obviate interference by the dons, to print and publish *The Granta* in London; the weekly issues of the periodical were sent to Cambridge every Saturday morning. At first a coloured cartoon of some prominent undergraduate was included, but this was not very successful and was soon abandoned. Mr Holland found himself under the necessity of devoting his time to some more serious object; Mr Guthrie tired of his new journalistic toy; and *The Granta* was made over, lock, stock and barrel, to a new Editor, who had already been partly responsible for it from the beginning. My first change was to remove the publication to Cambridge, where it has ever since remained. I was lucky enough to be able to get together a brilliant band of contributors, chief of whom was Barry Pain, whose *Canadian Canoe* and *Celestial Grocery* acquired for him celebrity that extended beyond the boundaries of Cambridge. After no long time we were able to pay our contributors and thus to strengthen a tendency to send MSS to *The Granta*.

One famous episode I must recall. It occurred to Geake, who was a Mathematical Fellow of Clare and at the same time assistant editor of *The Granta*, that it would be an excellent scoop for *The Granta* to publish on Saturday morning the solutions of the problem paper in the Mathematical Tripos which had been set on the previous day. He secured two high mathematicians to help him, and when the examination paper was available for the general public (at 9.30 a.m. on the Friday) he secured a copy of it and set his two tame mathematicians to work in an upper chamber at Clare. There I visited them once or twice, and there they finally accomplished their task. Geake stayed up till 5 o'clock in the morning in order to see the problem supplement through the press. At 10.30 a.m. it was on sale in Cambridge to the astonishment of all mathematicians, who were tremendously impressed by the fact that not merely three or four, but all the problems had been correctly solved. For me it was a great adventure amongst the signs and symbols of higher mathematics.

I have barely left myself space to congratulate you, Mr Editor, on your courage in reviving a paper which all have looked upon as dead. May you long continue in your task of viewing Cambridge life on its lighter side, an effort which was made impossible by the war, and which now lies fair before you.

1 May 1919

Professor Jebb in motion

23 February 1895

A Wail of Warning

F. ANSTEY

NOTE.—The following curious and instructive narrative has been deciphered from a document picked up by the Editor's gyp in a lane near Trinity Hall. We have decided to publish it, although we are by no means clear upon the precise application of the moral which its author would seem to intend, and we must decline to be responsible for the truth of any statements contained in the MS.

PORTION THE FIRST

I, FERDINAND FITKIN, formerly a member of this University,—now, alas! a denizen of the dungeon wherein I have languished for a term of years beyond my powers of computation—commit my painful story to writing under conditions most discouraging to sustained literary effort, as will be gathered from the fact that I am reduced to tracing these lines by stealth, and at long intervals, in shorthand, with the tongue of an old waistcoat-buckle and a bottle of secreted marking-ink, upon both sides of a paper collar, the sole surviving remnant of a once scrupulous regard for appearances. When the collar is full, I shall toss it through the bars of my cell, in the hope that haply it may reach a sympathetic hand. I have no personal ends to serve in making known the facts which led to my incarceration. Sympathy I cannot expect; freedom I have long ceased to desire. The protracted and enforced deprivation of all toilet requisites has rendered me unfit for any other society than that of the tame toad I have trained to be my companion. Ah me! the very toad, could it know the nature of the offence that brought me here, would shrink from me with unaffected loathing. But the space afforded to composition by a paper collar is limited. Let me be brief.

I am now undergoing imprisonment for having once—and here I would entreat those who may read this confession, to temper their condemnation with charity—for having once, many years ago, when still a happy and innocent Corpus Undergraduate, suffered myself to be led into assuming the editorship of an intercollegiate periodical. Such a proceeding would never have occurred to me but for the insidious persuasions of one whom I trusted implicitly as a friend—one Piffler, of Peterhouse. He painted our prospects in glowing colours; he absolutely proved to me that we *could* not drop more than a five-pound note per week apiece over our venture. To a non-literary man, like myself, the post of Editor offered temptations well-nigh irresistible. In a fatal moment of weakness I sent my gyp out for a copy of Webster's dictionary, and sank into the editorial chair of the *Cambridge Cockiolly Bird*. Such was the title of our paper, though I objected to it from the first as frivolous, there being no bird of that name known to British ornithology. But Piffler said the prospectus was already issued, and I was not to be an ass. The other members of our staff were Titmuss of Trinity, Caulker of Cats, and Diggle of Downing—all quiet and inoffensive men to outward appearance, with no indications of the deplorable tendencies to humour and sarcasm which they afterwards but too unmistakably evinced. I myself was under the impression that we were merely to report college sports and matches, speeches at the various boat clubs and debating societies, and the University sermon, with a column for original poetry and correspondence. I was genuinely horrified when I discovered that Piffler and his reckless associates were actually proposing to provide the University with an amusing periodical! Now I

was aware that the University, as a body, resents any attempt
to amuse it. Should it require entertainment, it has its humour
down in moderate quantities from town; but it can get on
perfectly well without it. However, though I represented this,
I was over-ruled, and I am ashamed to say that I had not
sufficient moral courage to withdraw, as I should have done.
Still, with all their presumption, they meant well, poor fellows! We were to be light and lively, smart and satirical, and
yet wound the feelings of none; our sarcasm should be
general, never particular. Accordingly, Titmuss evolved a
series of typical Undergraduates, whom he lashed, under
imaginary names, with the most scathing ridicule. Caulker,
having a pretty talent for pen-and-ink sketching, drew their
portraits, which, as they resembled nothing human, we did
not think likely to offend the most sensitive. Thus we hoped
our little *Cockiolly Bird* would chirp and twitter without ever
dropping the olive branch from its beak, or pecking one
friendly hand that took it in. For all that, our first number was
not well received. The men did not like its tone; it seemed to
them that, though we abstained from personalities, we treated
Undergraduates, as a class, without sufficient reverence, and
in a style of assumed superiority that was felt to be vaguely
offensive. We found it advisable to preserve a strict incognito;
notwithstanding which the men of Piffler's college—a sporting set—discovered his identity by an easy process of elimina-
tion, and treated him with marked coolness, carrying their
system of ostracism, indeed, to the extent of compelling him
to remain for a somewhat prolonged period under the spout
of the college pump.

Even this *contretempts*, however, did not damp Piffler; it
only led him to propose a change of tactics. In future, he said,
if we were to be popular, we must aim our harmless shafts at
Dons alone. To be sure, we knew less than nothing about
them; but that, as Titmuss pointed out, left us a freer hand.
Once more I demurred. I thought the Dons might possibly be

displeased; but at this Caulker came down upon me with burning indignation. Did I not know that the leading men in the land were travestied and caricatured every day in London comic papers? Were *they* displeased? Why, they were the first to join in the chorus of good-humoured laughter! And was it likely that the most learned and cultured members of our University would show a less keen sense of humour—a greater ignorance of the world? Very *well*, then!

I know now what miserable fallacies these were, but they sounded plausible enough at the time. As before, I was weak enough to give way, only stipulating that we should continue to confine our satire to types. Thereupon Titmuss set to work once more, and invented an impossible monstrosity—inflated, arrogant, pompous, tyrannical—in a word, the Don of tradition and convention. He called this abstraction Proudfoot, and in Proudfoot the entire staff, with the exception of myself, simply revelled. They pictured him in all conceivable situations, and invariably under some ludicrous aspect. Piffler reported imaginary and preposterous lectures by Proudfoot; Titmuss wrote a ribald scene representing Proudfoot conversing affably with his aged bedmaker; Diggle constructed ponderous epigrams and table-talk which he falsely ascribed to him; Caulker sketched him in a variety of more or less absurd positions. Proudfoot's furniture and habits, his walks on the Trumpington and Madingley roads, his deportment at college meetings—all these, and much more, were enlarged upon with loving elaboration. It was done in the purest innocence. As far as I know, the whole was sheer invention; there never *was* any Proudfoot; and yet, little as we dreamed of it, we were rushing blindly to our destruction! On the day that the second and last number of the *Cambridge Cockiolly Bird* appeared——

[The remainder of the MS, which is continued on the back of the collar, is not yet transcribed, but will appear in the next number of *The Granta*.—ED.]   *17 May 1889*

Women's Degrees

LEADING ARTICLE

The harpies are upon us, and this time with a vengeance. No longer can we regard the question of Women's Degrees from a calm and philosophic point of view. The time has passed for expressing pious opinions, and indulging in threadbare jests. Within a week or two a vote will be recorded in the Senate House which will affect the future of this University more than a score of Boat Races, and which will decide once and for all the lines on which the women of England are to be educated.

We do not wish to waste our readers' time, still less our own space, so we state at once that the present proposal to grant to women by diploma a titular B.A. can only be regarded by any reasonable man as an inevitable step towards a mixed University. Many of the leaders of the movement do not disguise that this is the goal towards which they would have us press. No other construction can be put on the letters in which the principals of Newnham and Girton addressed the Syndicate. Lest there should be any mistake at this point, let us consider the question in its logical bearing. It is asserted that an anomaly exists, that women who take a class in the Tripos are entitled to those letters which adorn the names of their rivals who take the London examination. We grant that this is an anomaly, an injustice, or anything else our opponents like to call it. How is it proposed to remove this anomaly? By creating another infinitely more serious, at any rate as far as the University of Cambridge is concerned. It is proposed that women should not only sit for our Honours examinations, that they should not only, to all intents and purposes, take our various degrees, that they should not only pay our fees, but that having been allowed so much as this, they should be excluded from any voice in the Government of the University. This is anomaly with a vengeance; so much so that we would emphasise in the strongest terms the conviction previously stated, that if the titular degree be granted, such an agitation will be set on foot as will render it impossible for the authorities to refuse women full membership.

What, then, are the reasons against full membership? They are so numerous that it is scarcely possible to state them with brevity. To begin with, five out of every six junior men are opposed to the scheme. These form the class on which the University entirely depends. These too are the men who will suffer most. So long as the scheme is so exceedingly unpopular among the rank and file of the University, it would be utter folly on the part of the Senate to take this irreversible step at the bidding of a small majority of a Syndicate, chosen as we all know how Syndicates are chosen. Again, the University Lecture Rooms and Laboratories are crowded enough in all conscience, and we should have thought that any man of sense would see that a large number of subjects do not lend themselves to treatment in mixed classes. Moreover, the whole scheme is of the nature of an experiment. There is no instance, ancient or modern, of a mixed, resident University such as these educational speculators desire Cambridge to be. Why should a University, which stands second to none either in this or any other country, be subjected to utterly tentative exploitation?

Nor do we regard this subject from only one point of view. Grant that you have drawn up on paper the constitution of a mixed University, what is it in reality? As at present, the men's colleges will always have to be separated from the

women's colleges by an impassable gulf of rules and regula-
tions. So far as athletics and those social influences go which
make the great Universities what they are, women and men
will live entirely distinct lives. No enthusiast—however he
may scheme and plot and organise—can create a real bond
between the two sets of colleges. All he can ensure is that
they shall mutually hamper each other.

The present scheme threatens the prosperity not only of
our University—and thank heaven, it *is* still ours—but of
women's education. We agree that women should take a
degree. What we advise is that they should grant their own
degree. We believe that women are not undeveloped men.
Our opponents say they are, but our opponents say a good
many foolish things. And, moreover, we believe that women
have a character, not identical with, but complementary to
that which we, who are men, possess. This being so, we think
that it is absurd to imagine that an intellectual training which
is exactly suited to men's requirements will be exactly suited
to women's requirements. If it suits men it will not suit
women. If it suits women, it will not suit men. The result of
an attempt to identify the opposed, will be a compromise,
which will permanently injure that future of women's education, which has been endangered enough already by the
impatient folly of those who try to do a century's work in a
week of garrulity and pamphleteering. And, moreover, such
a compromise will not fail to detract from that unsurpassed—
we might almost say unrivalled—reputation which Cambridge
possesses as the pioneer in accurate and scientific thought.

24 April 1897

A Dream of the Future

29 February 1896

The Tragedy of Biggs

A. A. MILNE

There once was a Fresher called Biggs—
  Who attended a lecture on statics
      (but only 'electro-')
      With a very correct row
Of friends who adored Mathematics,
              In Attics,
And hated all forms of Aquatics!

Now he learnt, in a very short time,
  How 'electric conductors' would—swear
      When 'charged by the force'
      (That's a policeman of course)
With wilfully seeking to cram
              In his tram
A motor, six bikes, and a pram.

Then 'a sphere in a uniform field'—
  And the way that it commonly rolls—
      And 'the energy shown:'
      They were no more unknown
Than 'a couple of opposite poles,'
              —Which are goals;
(And 'circular currents'—in shoals).

A. A. Milne

But the problems of 'infinite space'
   Was a thing he but knew by renown;
     And he swore—by the moon!
     He'd 'get into it' soon!—
He would learn it before he went down
       Ho! Ho!
He will learn it before he comes down!

For the gas was escaping one night—
   With a candle he looked for the place!

    Well, he left for the sun
    At a quarter to one;
And he seemed to be in for a race
      By the pace
That he soared up to infinite space!

And he hopes to get into it soon!
   (Forgive me for dropping a tear)
     On Friday at noon
     He had passed by the moon,
And was making for Saturn, I hear;
      Which is near—
So he ought to be there in a year.

2 November 1901

The Complete Novel Writer

A. A. MILNE

First of all, a title. So much advice has been given on this subject that I propose to say only a few words. The important thing to remember is this: Your title must have no meaning. Suppose you select *Grape-Nuts*. Then *Grape-Nuts* may be the family name of the heroine, or her pet name for the hero, or it may have some subtle meaning like *Wormwood*. Anyhow it will be a pleasant puzzle for your readers to discover where the Grape-Nuts come in; and if, in the end, it turns out to be an advertisement then it will be somewhat in the nature of a surprise to them. Another popular class of title takes the form of a question, *Ought she to have done it? Did he expect it from her?* In this case your novel will devote itself to answering the question in some hundred pages. If you and your public discover that she most certainly ought not to have done it, then in your new edition you may change the title to *How was it she didn't do it, supposing, for the moment, that she ought to have done it?*

There may not be room to get all this in on the back, so call it *A Wayward Woman* for short.

Having selected a title for the book, the next thing is to find one for the hero. Call him Lord Walton-on-the-Naze, if you like; but don't specify whether he is a viscount or a baron or an earl or anything else. It really isn't safe. You had better make all your characters of noble birth. It may seem strange at first for your bootboy to be a retired Duke, but he

B

will get used to it and so will you. When your foreign Prince (don't let him be English, or they will identify him and run you in for libel) wants to murder someone *incog.* let him disguise himself as a baronet. It is so much more genteel.

Now you are ready to begin.

Chapter I

The first chapter must describe an old country house 'in the most beautiful corner of Blankshire'. Any guide book will do. Kenilworth Castle and Hampton Court Maze between them should give you all you want. Don't mention any of the characters until the last few lines. Then finish up like this: 'Such was the scene that spread itself before the eyes of the youthful Lord Fitz Badly in the glamour of a golden evening towards the middle of June some twenty years ago; perhaps the fairest scene that mortal eye had ever gazed upon since the days when . . .'

Don't describe Lord F. B. You won't want him again. And no one else will. This brings us to

Chapter II

Start with a new character. 'Lord Grasmere was a middle-aged man of some thirty summers.' When you have been all over him, from the way he parts his hair down to the town address of his bootmaker, then leave him and pick up someone else. Let it be a lady. Describe her and let them talk. Let them talk in the ordinary way that two such people would *not* talk in, but finish up like this if you can.

'At this moment a man rose from his chair and glided noiselessly out of the room. Lady Dorothy got up hastily and held her breath.

"Do you know who that is?" she whispered.

"No, do you?"

"*It is John Bloggs!*" '

Don't mention John Bloggs again.

Chapter III

'When Lord Henry Dent de lion went down from Cambridge with a third-class in History and a reputation for bad cigars, not even his best friends thought . . .' Describe him. You might almost be funny at the expense of Lord Henry. Say that 'those who saw him, for the first time, told themselves that after all there might be something in the Darwinian theory'. It is neither original, nor humorous, nor remarkable for its good taste—but never mind that.

Having said all you want to about Lord Henry, put him away somewhere where you will know him again. He may come in useful later on. You can always refer to his features when you feel in a humorous vein. By the way, Lord Henry might be a second cousin on his mother's side to the Prince Aloyau de Bœuf. Haven't you mentioned him? Then do it now.

Chapter IV

'Prince Aloyau de Bœuf was as handsome as he was highborn. His friends called him familiarly "Prince"'—this was rather original of them, all things considered—'and his nickname suited him. For he *was* a Prince.' (You have just said so before, of course, but there is no harm in repeating it. You don't meet a Prince every day of your life.)

Be very careful as to the way you describe him. When you have finished, leave him till Chapter XV. In Chapter XV important developments take place, and you will want all the spare royalty you can lay hands on.

For the next nine chapters, introduce as many new characters as you can. Always start a chapter with a new one, and then end it with another, if possible. This brings us to

Chapter XIV

A new character. The aged King of Malaria, dying of asthma. Also his son, the youthful Prince Consort. Don't describe either of them. The next chapter is twenty years later in point of time, and in twenty years the King will be dead, and his son so much altered that it wouldn't be much use wasting time over him now, would it?

When you had finished raving over his beautiful chestnut hair, your readers would have turned over the page and discovered him, with his iron grey locks, in

Chapter XV—*Twenty Years After*

By this time you have some twenty members of the aristocracy present—and John Bloggs. But you won't want him. Begin like this:—

'It was the Fancy Dress Ball of the season, and the Duchess of Billingsgate was waiting at the head of the kitchen-stair to receive her guests. Among the more notable people present were——' (then run through your characters again). 'Little did any of them think that this night was fraught with dreadful possibilities for more than one of them.'

At this point collect all your MS, tie it up in a parcel and send it to any respectable home for the incurable blind. It wouldn't be much fun going on.

3 May 1902

The Sunshade

IAN HAY

I am very much annoyed with Mopson. I am also annoyed in a lesser degree with Miss Pansy Crumpit; also, though in a different way, with myself. But chiefly with Mopson, for I feel that I can never get quite even with him again.

However, I will tell the story from the beginning, and the judicious reader shall apportion for himself the responsibility for the deplorable catastrophe which has occurred.

I

Mopson and I live on the same staircase. He is several years my junior—two, to be precise, he being a Freshman and I practically a B.A. He is the son of our rector at home, and when his parents brought him to the College at the beginning of the term I faithfully promised his father that I would not lend Mopson money, and his mother that I would protect Mopson from undesirable influences.

I introduced Mopson to three of my most intimate friends—Allnutt, who is making rather a stir in the chess world just now; Mugby, the only undergraduate (to my knowledge) who has ever been invited to go for a walk with our College Tutor; and Spottisford, whom we in our little circle call 'The Blood', because he is so fastidious about his appearance and personal comforts. He flatly declines to wear a turn-down collar on week-days, and there is practically only one brand of cocoa which he will drink.

Each of my friends tried to do something for Mopson. On one occasion he visited the Fitzwilliam Museum in company with Mugby, and on another Allnutt took him to a visitors' night at the Chess Club. Spottisford, knowing that young blood sometimes runs hotly, took him to a rather rowdy meeting of the Theological Society. Several times we allowed him to accompany us upon our tri-weekly jaunt to Grantchester, and one night we took him to hear us ring ten thousand variations on the triple bob major at the weekly gathering of the Change Ringing Guild.

Few undergraduates enter the whirl of academic life under such tutelage as this; but Mopson proved to be absolutely impervious to civilisation. As Mugby well said, he was 'impossible'. He was docile enough for a week or two. Then, one morning he dropped into my room, and announced that although I wasn't a bad old buffer myself, my friends struck him as the 'absolute terminus'. Condescending to details, he criticised Spottisford's—*Spottisford's!*—dress, and added that two men who solemnly posted Cicero's Letters to one another for purposes of perusal at breakfast, as Allnutt and Mugby were in the habit of doing, were only fit to go and play at rabbits in an asylum for criminal lunatics. He concluded by imploring me as a personal favour to purchase an india-rubber and erase the lot.

I kept my temper, as I always do, and presently Mopson left the room, banging the door behind him. Next day I encountered a boy on the staircase labouring under a basket containing bottles of lager beer, and later in the day a nauseating stench from the upper regions apprised me of the fact that Mopson had purchased a box of cigars and set up as a smoker.

Not content with thus ostentatiously burning his boats, Mopson proceeded to advertise his emancipation from my guardianship in a more concrete fashion. I found myself coerced into a sort of guerrilla warfare.

I have a habit of pinning up notices of anything I may require for breakfast outside my oak overnight, to attract the somewhat unobservant eye of my bedmaker, Mrs Gunn, when she arrives in the morning. On the Saturday evening following my rupture with Mopson, since I was expecting three friends to breakfast, I wrote upon a scrap of paper : —

> Please get me
> 12 eggs.

and pinned it outside the door as usual. Next morning Mrs Gunn, whom a life spent in the society of irresponsible youth has robbed of all sense of proportion or capacity for surprise, protruded her bonneted head into my bedroom and observed : —

'*Begging* your pardon, sir, but the Kitchens is sorry they can't give you more than seventy-four 'ens' eggs this morning. But they are sending up a couple of dozen ducks' eggs as well. in case they should be any use.'

Mopson, on his way up to bed the night before, had added a 0 to my 12!

It was the first shot in a long campaign. I rose, put on a dressing-gown, picked my way through a sea of eggs, and went upstairs to interview Mopson. His door was sported, but on a covered dish left outside by a kitchen-man I observed three slices of cold beef—Mopson's lunch. Evidently he had given up having breakfast on Sunday mornings—another step in the downward path. I returned to my room and procured a large envelope, which I inscribed, rather aptly, I think : —'One of Cicero's Letters!' Into this I slipped Mopson's slices of beef, and posted it in Mopson's letter-box. Then I went downstairs again, feeling better.

The war raged for some weeks, but I will not weary the

reader with a description of Mopson's somewhat dubious
methods of conducting it. A single example will suffice. One
morning, on returning to my rooms from a lecture, I was surprised to find a group of men standing about in the court outside my staircase, looking upward and smiling. My glasses are
not suited to long-distance reading, and I was thus unable to
distinguish what was printed on a placard, fixed to the wall
some way up. On getting upstairs to my room I found that
Mopson had forced an entrance and hung out from my
window a large notice with the following legend:—

```
WASHING!
A MANGLE KEPT
HEAR!
```

I retaliated by deleting Mopson's name from the Candidates'
Book of our Coptic Manuscripts Club, for which I had put him
up previous to our disagreement. I wrote him a note to that
effect, and he wrote back recommending me to starch my
dickey.

This is the first part of the story.

II

After this we did not speak to one another for a whole
term. And then, somewhat to my surprise, Mopson made an
effort at reconciliation.

One evening I encountered him at the door of the Union. I
was coming out of a Private Business Meeting, and Mopson
had come in to read the racing telegrams. These telegrams, by
the way, I regard as a most pernicious institution. Times
without number have I drawn the attention of the Vice-
President to their demoralising influence upon people like
Mopson. Once I put down a strongly-worded motion for
debate upon the subject. But I need hardly say that no one

could be found bold enough to oppose me; so something of a more controversial nature was substituted, and my motion was shelved.

Anyhow, I met Mopson. He addressed me in a somewhat shamefaced and awkward manner.

'Look here, Oyler, old man,' he said, 'I'm afraid I've been giving you a rotten time lately. I *have* been overdoing it a bit, and that's a fact. But you know what a blighter I am. I don't mean any harm. Anyhow, I'm sorry—there! Come and have a drink at the "Gazeka".'

I was never one to bear malice, and said so. I then accepted his apology. As regards his offer of refreshment, I replied, as he must have expected me to reply, that I was an abstainer. He merely replied:—'Well, come and see *me* put one away, old son, and you can have a chat with Pansy.'

I went—not, of course, because I was allured by the mention of Pansy, but because I remembered my promise to Mopson's mother.

Pansy proved to be a young person of considerable but somewhat mature attractions, in a purple blouse. Mopson, evidently with the intention of impressing me, ordered the most difficult liqueur he could think of, and then effected an introduction between myself and the lady. I attempted one or two conversational openings of a nature which I considered suitable to her intellectual standard, only to be interrupted with the somewhat irrelevant request that I would not address her as Miss Crumpit.

'Call me Pansy,' said the lady. 'I don't like being called Crumpit. It makes me feel like somethink to eat!'

'So you are!' exclaimed the infatuated Mopson.

'Naughty boy!' replied Miss Crumpit, archly rapping him on the knuckles with a stone match-stand.

Mopson retaliated by picking up the match-stand and emptying its contents over the mop-like *coiffure* of Miss Crumpit. In the playful scuffle which then ensued my toe was trodden on, and Miss Crumpit's little finger suffered abrasion through contact with the safety-pin which fastened the corners of Mopson's collar together. (She was endeavouring to pull his tie out by the roots at the moment.) Mopson offered no apology in the matter of my toe, but insisted on applying first-aid (of a kind unrecognised in the medical profession) to the lady's little finger before we left.

That is the second part of the story. It merely serves to introduce Miss Crumpit to the reader's notice.

III

I regret to say that by the beginning of the May Term the armistice between myself and Mopson had come to an end. Possibly I was a little nasty in writing to Mopson's parents about Miss Pansy Crumpit, but Mopson was certainly not justified in calling me a canting hypocrite and addressing me as 'Stiggins' and 'Pecksniff' whenever we met on the staircase.

As many of my readers are aware, Whitsuntide at Cambridge used to be made hideous by the arrival of innumerable showmen's caravans upon Midsummer Common, where a fair of the most undesirable type was set going. One evening after hall Spottisford and I took a stroll in this direction. We had no intention of participating in any of the amusements provided, but the contemplation of humanity, however debased, must always be of interest to a thoughtful man.

Spottisford and I, then, wandered round the fair amid the flare of lights and medley of mechanically produced noises, resisting the blandishments of gentlemen in charge of swing-boats and ladies who desired us to project missiles at coconuts. I was sorry to observe a large number of undergraduates present, all mingling freely with the roughs and shop-girls of the town, and treating the latter to all the amusements the place could offer. I pointed this out to Spottisford, and we were both animadverting somewhat sharply on the absence of the Proctors, when—we came face to face with Mopson

and Miss Pansy Crumpit, arm-in-arm! Miss Crumpit still wore
the purple blouse, but the most conspicuous article of her
outfit was a scarlet sunshade, furled at the moment and
employed as a walking-stick. With the ferrule of this weapon,
as soon as she recognised me, she proceeded to dig me playfully in the ribs, enquiring at the same time whether I had
been writing home to mother lately.

I kept my temper. I removed the point of the sunshade from
the interstices of my ribs, and held it firmly aloof while I
spoke to Miss Crumpit. I pointed out in a clear and command-
ing voice—for it seemed to me that there were many present
who might benefit by listening to my homily—that she would
be much better employed even in dispensing inferior alcohol
across the bar of the 'Gazeka' than in trapesing about with a
mere child like Mopson.

Then I turned to Mopson, and was proceeding to read him
a sharp lecture—sadly interrupted, I fear, by a withering fire
of reflections upon my appearance and character from Miss
Crumpit—when there was a rush and a swirl in the unregenerate crowd which had gathered around us, accompanied
by a frantic cry of 'Proggins!'

Next moment everybody seemed to fade away. Mopson
vanished into space. Miss Crumpit was swallowed up by the
crowd. Even Spottisford, whom I thought I could have relied
on, was no longer at my side. Instead, I found myself confronted by a grim-looking gentleman in a cap and gown and
bands, behind whom stood two of the most ferocious-looking
myrmidons I have ever beheld. Thirty yards away I could see
another Proctor with his bulldogs, driving the crowd before
him.

There was a death-like silence. Even the steam organs
seemed to have stopped of their own accord.

The Proctor took off his hat, and enquired formally:—

'Your name and College, sir?'

It was a horrible position. Here was I, in the act of snatching a brand from the burning, actually mistaken by this un-discerning and hide-bound official for an opponent instead of an abettor of law and order. Of course, my character could be cleared. The College authorities would have nothing but this fellow's word to go upon, and my previous record would entirely absolve me from any charges which might be brought against me. Still, he seemed to be expecting some sort of explanation.

'Your name and——,' he began again.

I immediately proceeded, as succinctly as possible, to out-line the facts of the case for him. He was a man of no breed-ing and slight patience, for he presently interrupted me.

'Quite so,' he said—'*quite* so! But let me advise you, sir, when you go walking out with your lady friends, to return them their property before you part company. It makes subsequent explanations of your conduct so much more plausible.'

One of the bull-dogs guffawed suddenly, and, with a slowly sinking sensation at my heart and a slight tightening of the hair upon my scalp, I followed with my eye the direction of his gaze. Then I perceived the trap into which, whether it had been set by accident or design, I had fallen.

My right hand was still convulsively grasping the scarlet sunshade of Miss Pansy Crumpit!

The College authorities took a lenient view of the case. But I have been expelled from the Chess Club. Mopson has bought a bundle of tracts, and drops one into my letter-box every time he passes.

11 June 1909

Love Virginal

Lines for *Le Bout du Sillon* by Felicien Rops

DERMOT FREYER

The labour of the fields is hard:
    Who would subdue the stubborn earth
    Must first subdue himself; from birth
Of day till dark without reward

He must endure. Even as one
    Of his own beasts he must become . . .
    Dull-eyed, dark-featured, patient, dumb;
Strong simple servant of the sun.

For him the music of the wood
    In May on heedless ears must fall;
    On sightless eyes the carnival
Of summer over field and flood.

But when love comes! Ah, when love comes,
    For him no fetters bid him stay,
    No thorns of thought counsel delay
When pulses beat like battle drums.

For him it is the cry, the call
    Of the great mother, merciless;
    O Love! untame'd arbitress,
Full-blooded, pulsing, virginal!

11 June 1912

Those in Authority

MR RUPERT BROOKE (King's College)
President of the Cambridge University
Fabian Society

Rupert Brooke came into residence at Cambridge in October 1906. The populace first became aware of him when they went to see the Greek Play of that year, *The Eumenides*, and many of them have not yet forgotten his playing of the Herald.

He brought with him to Cambridge a reputation both as an athlete and as a poet, a combination supposed by vulgar people to be impossible.

He represented Rugby at cricket and football, rose to high rank in the Volunteer Corps, and was not unknown as a steeplechaser. He also won a prize poem.

There is a vacant place reserved for him between Matthew Arnold and Arthur Hugh Clough, in the Poets' Corner in Rugby School Chapel.

At Cambridge he has forsaken a few old fields and entered many new ones. While a Freshman he used on occasions to represent his college in various branches of athletics, but soon dropped the habit, in spite of protests. On his day he is still an irrestible tennis player, preferring to play barefooted, and to pick up the balls with his toes.

As an actor *The Eumenides* provided him with not his only triumph. He was one of the founders of the Marlowe Dramatic Society, which still flourishes, and among his later successes may be counted his performances in Marlowe's *Faustus* and in *Comus* during the Milton celebrations.

He has continued to write poems, some of which should be familiar to readers of the *Westminster Gazette* and *The Cambridge Review*. But the rest and certain other writings, not in verse, are known as yet only to a few, and mainly to certain King's Societies of which he is a member.

Some of us hope that the world will one day know more of them.

He is also a politician. His public utterances have indeed been few, though he once made a speech at the joint meeting of the Fabian Society and the Liberal Club, which two ex-presidents of the Union may still remember. But public speaking is not the only function of the politician, though the contrary opinion is sometimes held. For two years he has been a prominent member of the Fabian Society, of which he is now President. He is sometimes credited with having started a new fashion in dress, the chief features of which are the absence of collars and headgear and the continual wearing of slippers.

He will tell you that he did not really begin to live till he went out of college at the end of his third year and took up his residence at 'The Orchard,' Grantchester.

It is said that there he lives the rustic life, broken by occasional visits to Cambridge; that he keeps poultry and a cow, plays simple tunes on a pan pipe, bathes every evening at sunset, and takes all his meals in a rose garden.

5 February 1910

Musical Notes: the Melba Concert

J.B.B.

When listening to a singer of such extraordinary natural gifts as Madame Melba, one loses the faculty of criticism for the time being in the appreciation of a wealth of sound that is in itself entirely enchanting.

On Wednesday evening the audience was taken irresistibly out of itself by the appeal of the glorious voice, and one felt more than ever convinced of the astounding influence wielded by a great vocalist on the average person, an influence immeasurably greater than that of any instrumentalist, however masterly.

Nearly all the great music of the world is instrumental, and all the great masters have clothed their profoundest utterances in the rich robes of orchestration. But the understanding of such works is reserved for the few, while the sensitiveness of a great voice for its own sake is common to very nearly everybody.

Madame Melba was most amazing and exhilarating in the dramatic excerpts, especially the Mad Scene from Lucia, but it was in the simple things such as Tosti's 'Goodbye' that she really touched the people.

Now the simple songs she sang were practically all of them bad in themselves, and one is confronted with the puzzling but undoubted fact that a great singer makes his or her deepest impression by singing songs of common-place and vulgar sentiment. This is to be regretted, though probably time will bring an improvement, as the musical tastes and understanding of the English are rapidly developing.

Mr Edmund Burke has a very fine rich baritone voice, the use of which he thoroughly understands.

Why, however, did he sing Schumann's 'Two Grenadiers' in French, which language is ridiculously unsuitable for this song? 'God Save the King' might be rendered in Chinese from the point of view of variety, but it would perhaps lose in some other respects.

We thoroughly enjoyed Moussorgsky's song about the flea, which Mr Burke sang with great spirit and crispness.

Miss Una Bourne has good technique, but made little impression on us as an interpreter, especially as she had handicapped herself so much in her choice of pieces.

The flute player, Mr Marcel Moyse, was very agreeable to listen to, and a finished performer; but a flute soon becomes wearisome, as there is so little variety possible. The Handel Allegro was very lively and enjoyable.

There was not as good an audience as there might have been, but those who did not go because of their disappointment in the Corn Exchange, when Madame Melba could not do herself justice, lost a delightful evening.

22 February 1913

Ragging at the Theatre

JACK HULBERT

It is an amazing thing, but in this highly civilised age every man has to earn his own living. Each person slaves in a particular line of business, according to his birth or social position. The struggle for existence in many cases renders choice impossible. The present generation is forced to take what chance provides, and that is partly why we have so many bad actors, entirely devoid of talent. Acting or farming is usually the last resource of those who have failed at everything else.

The people who lack money, education, and opportunity should at least evoke our pity. Numbers of these come up here in small touring companies, invariably bullied by the smaller, uncultured stage manager, who, as often as not, is a perfect tyrant without reserve. These touring people look forward to their visit to Cambridge, counting the days like children, and cherish the greatest expectations, only to find, perhaps, that a highly educated audience has not a grain of sympathy.

Take another view. The University is supposed to turn out her men 'hall marked', but her success will not be very greatly enhanced by men continually giving vent to their 'after-dinner' sensations by rolling into the Theatre and misbehaving themselves in public. The privacy of a College court, not the theatre, is surely better fitted for such frivolity. This sort of thing is not done in May Week, because there are so many ladies about; but all the year round ladies are present at the theatre. This fact seems to be overlooked.

Having briefly reviewed these two sides of the question—the struggling actor and the indiscreet undergraduate—let us try and consider what actually takes place.

As the curtain rises a *small* number of undergraduates are already in their seats. These have come oddly enough to see the piece—and listen. When the first act is half over a few more troop in. These have come to see what remarks they can make—and shout. Sometime later, when they have sat down, and when their subdued laughter has died away, the wretched performers begin to make themselves heard once more, and so do part of the audience, with some exceedingly subtle repartee as the following:—

The Actor: 'I love you.'
Audience: 'Swish.'
Actor: 'I must kiss—.'
Audience: Cork noise.
Actor: 'Oh, I can't bear to leave you.'
Audience: 'You're a sportsman, sir.'
Actress: 'I can't let you go, I love *you*, too.'
Audience: 'Wow-wow.'

Now, from an unprejudiced point of view, are these remarks really clever, or are they simply manifestations of the type of man who makes them? One is led to believe that they originate in order to provide fuel for the raging furnace of cheap notoriety. When a fresher comes up he, naturally, wants to make good use of his newly-acquired freedom, and make a hit in this University; but paying half-a-crown to interfere with people, who, unlike himself, are struggling to earn their living, is not going to crown him with honours.

Theatrical people have the emotional element as strongly marked in them as in other human beings. No man is helped up the mountain side of toil by undue ragging. The feelings of a person of low birth are more deeply wounded by the unkind act of his superiors than by one of his own class.

In some companies a series of bad press notices will get a man the sack. But an actor could not have a worse notice than to be ragged by the public.

It is hard to avoid the fact that it is a cowardly thing to sit in a comfortable chair, adding another pair of glaring eyes to the public gaze and interrupt, *ad lib.*, people who are straining themselves to entertain some hundreds of critical spectators—it is an unpleasant ordeal, if the part is a difficult one. The feeling of standing on the stage, and beholding through a veil of dazzling light the dim outline of a sea of faces, is inclined to be disconcerting. There are already enough difficulties behind the scenes to upset anyone's nerves, without having them increased by the audience.

If bad shows are booked for this theatre the *actors* are not the people to be blamed; they are, naturally, trying to do their best—give them a sporting chance.

As a concluding note, let it be impressed upon those who are unconvinced that yearning for cheap notoriety, misbehaving oneself before ladies, and crushing the feelings of people who are struggling to make both ends meet, is called 'ragging at the theatre'.

1 March 1913

Rugger Reminiscences
by an International
(W. W. WAKEFIELD)

What can a fellow do when the Editor beards him in bed and says: 'My lad, we want some Rugger reminiscences from you'? What one did was to give him something to reminisce about by asking him this: 'What would you do if in the 'Varsity match just as you were off, on a clear half-way run down the field somebody ripped your shorts off?' He was heard to go away remarking: 'A delicate situation.' And so it is, believe me.

It is strange how different impressions are left with one about the various International matches. For instance, in Wales the main impression left is Mud, a babble of unintelligible tongues, the weird singing of 'Land of my Fathers' by 40,000 people, and some very large forwards with large grasping hands and feet to match. The impressions of an Irish match in Ireland are entirely different. Everything is forgotten in face of that nasty little bit of water which is between. All that can be conjured up is a vision (both ways) of 'faces in front of one, faces to right of one, faces to left of one,' all looking very unhappy, some lying on deck, some evidently trying to hear what the wild waves are saying. Try how one might, that is all one can visualise—bombs, Sinn Feiners, Black and Tans, and all the rest fade before such a vision.

Now, on the other hand, the Scotch match leaves happier memories. One remembers seeing (and feeling) a lot of big boots with mud on; also one felt a nasty cold wind—funny people to live in such a climate—but this is supplemented by Haggis and the Accessory, and the memory of a long, long lane that seems to have no ending (luckily very broad), sometimes called Princes Street. Yes, certainly a happier memory.

And now we come to the French match. Immediately a word forms, and that word is PARIS. And the funny part about it is (although on second thoughts considering the circumstances perhaps it isn't so funny) if you ask anyone about the match in Paris, whether he played in it or saw it, and this applies to other matches as well, he will invariably answer by saying: 'I lost sight of so and so after 1 a.m.; do you know where he went to?' Or, 'I got as far as the "Casino".'

But never a word about the match, O ye London and kindred teams so full of 'Varsity players.

Strange reminiscences of Football you will doubtless say, dear reader, but nevertheless very, very true.

Quite a lot of fun takes place in touring too. Touring sides are not apt to take the football too seriously, although the home side invariably does, and not always in the right way either.

To wit:—Once when touring in the west country we kicked off against a strong wind. The ball was very light and pointed, and the local side again and again made ground galore with long kicks down wind. However, at half time we were leading, so when they kicked off we renewed with stout hearts. But oh, the ball they kicked off with; round, heavy, and tubby, and whenever it was kicked it didn't seem to make much difference whether it was against or with the wind. The result was they beat us. After the game it struck our captain to ask why the balls were changed. Their captain, a hoary old veteran, with a wink and a nudge, said: 'I haven't been playing football for 25 years without learning a thing or two!'

You try it, and you will see why the balls were changed.

One well-known side which goes on tour in cars every year has a beer barrel car with it; strange, but they generally win their matches! We understand that the 'Varsity side have already tried to get a truck or van large enough for their barrel, but have so far failed. But, thanks to *The Granta* and the Washington Conference, the many thousands of Admiralty unemployed have now a job, and a satisfactory receptacle will be on the Euston train on the morning of the ninth.

About fifteen years ago Wales played the New Zealanders, and were the only team to beat them, which they did by a try amid great enthusiasm. After the match the following incident took place on the playing pitch between two miners:—

'It was here, mon, I tell you.'

'Are you sure it was here, Evan?'

'Indeed, mon, with mine own eyes I saw him put the ball there.'

'Indeed to goodness it must be so then.'

And he took a spade from under his coat and proceeded to cut away a sod which he carefully wrapped up and bore off in triumph to his native village in the mountains, there to show his admiring friends the piece of turf on which the try was scored for Wales when the New Zealanders were beaten.

Implements ready, chaps, for Twickenham on the 8th, and we'll order a special train to take the turf from Liverpool Street!

30 November 1921

A First Purpose of the English Tripos

SIR ARTHUR QUILLER-COUCH

> If he engages in controversy of any kind, his
> disciplined intellect preserves him from the
> blundering discourtesy of better, perhaps, but less
> educated minds; who, like blunt weapons, tear and
> hack instead of cutting clean, who mistake the
> point in argument, waste their strength on trifles,
> misconceive their adversary, and leave the ques-
> tion more involved than they find it.—*Cardinal
> Newman*.

An innocent and fairly obvious remark of mine, dropped
casually in a lecture—to the effect that a total abstainer,
without knowledge of wine, could not understand certain
felicitous passages in certain great authors—was snatched the
other day, from an abbreviated report and so twisted by
Prohibitionists out of its straight meaning that I soon found
myself under a suspicion of preaching that no one but a
habitual drunkard could appreciate *Hamlet*. It then but
required a zealot to suggest my expulsion from Cambridge as
a wanton elder, encouraging Undergraduates to 'drink': and
he was duly forthcoming.

In a previous lecture I had hinted a doubt that Anglo-
Saxon poetry is not very good poetry, and that Anglo-Saxon
prose (or the remains preserved to us) scarcely deserves to be
called prose at all. Now in this opinion I may, let us say, be
as easily wrong as right. But a Professor of London University
takes me up, slides the perfectly definite word 'Anglo-Saxon'

into 'Medieval', by loose alternation of these two terms makes me out a contemner of medieval literature (which I worship); and by extending *his* meaning of 'medieval' to Spenser, implies somehow that I must have a poor opinion of *The Faerie Queene.*

The other day, in *The Times*, an Anglican bishop wrote a letter or two on Divorce Reform. So far as I could interpret him I happened to agree with him. But his letters were couched in English so vilely uneducated that one was forced to doubt if his lordship had ever been at the expense of defining an impulse, through thought, into speech.

Now with these three examples before me I wonder if folk can ever be persuaded that clean thinking is a precedent of clean writing; that you cannot have the second without the first; and that to cultivate the two together is the first aim of our Tripos.

It sometimes seems quite hopeless to preach this doctrine. For the examples I have quoted are merely 'phenomenal' : the Prohibitionist, the Professor and the Bishop all write as they do, confusing thought, because in their youth they were never disciplined to define their terms. But when we find a like, or a worse, licence persisting in these days, after many Chairs have been founded as pulpits of English in many Universities, we may fairly suspect a real disease.

It exists; and at the root of it we touch, as usual, the malignant growth of a vested interest. So long as we elect Professors who cannot handle the extremely difficult business of writing their mother tongue, so long shall we have Professors who dodge back into corners where it is worth few people's while to detect them, and pretend, even of philology, that our language ceased to change in the fifteenth century, or at any rate that no subsequent changes deserve our attention : whereas the changes in our mere language since Shakespeare's time, and even the changes of idiom at this moment happening, deserve it more; while to continue the tradition of sound English thought expressed in sound English prose deserves it infinitely more.

But the professional teacher is, in my experience, unteachable. He retreats into his hole of vowel-endings, versecountings and writings which he can the more hardily allege to be of first importance in proportion as a scholar moderately acquainted with the classics finds them scarcely tolerable: and out of this retreat he will denounce you Sainte-Beuve, Arnold, Renan, Lemaître, or any of that gang.

I have before me a vision of such a Professor criticising our Tripos, and in my ears a recollection of some such dialogue as this in a Committee at Whitehall.

PROFESSOR: 'But Mr Chairman, I have studied a paper set in this Cambridge Tripos on the period 1350-1603; and I find a question set upon Guilds, another upon Architecture and a third on the Monasteries. Now what has either of these to do with English Language and Literature?'

RESPONDENT: 'Possibly a great deal. But ours is not a "Tripos of English Language and Literature". It is an "English Tripos".'

PROFESSOR: 'What is the difference?'

RESPONDENT: 'Well, in this particular paper we hope to find out what our men know about English literature, life and thought between 1350 and 1603. Our rule defines it as "Literature, life and thought": and, since we set eighteen questions and request the candidate to choose five, we allow his knowledge or ignorance some range. We desire to test his knowledge, not to examine his ignorance.'

PROFESSOR: 'But, Mr Chairman, here is a question on Architecture!'

CHAIRMAN: 'One question out of eighteen. The candidate is not forced to attempt it.'

PROFESSOR: 'But what, Sir, has a question on the styles of architecture to do with English Language and Literature?'

RESPONDENT: (wearily) 'The Professor, Sir, mistakes the very name of our Tripos. It is not a tripos of "English Language and Literature"; but an English Tripos. We think that English architecture bears most importantly on English life and thought between 1350 and 1603.'

PROFESSOR: 'It may be, Sir. But here is a paper set upon English Language and Literature in this capriciously chosen period—'

RESPONDENT: 'Forgive me, Sir; *not* upon "English Language and Literature".'

PROFESSOR: '—And, if the Committee will credit it, not a single question upon *Ferrex and Porrex!*'

If, then, our first purpose—or at any rate one of our main purposes—be to teach men to think and write with clarity and precision, it follows that our Tripos must be difficult; that we have little use for 'duds', for Tutors who misconceive it as being a soft option (and by consequence decoy the duckling to his doom), or for strange Professors who criticise it in terms of their own ideal constructions. At Oxford the Honours School of English claims that its 'first' is harder to win than a 'first' in any other School there, with the disputable exception of Greats. I have examined there, and here, and have assured myself that our standard in Cambridge is no lower: and, already the work of several of our few first-class men—work in criticism especially—is being eagerly taken by London Editors.

2 March 1923

Gladys Cooper in Diplomacy

CECIL BEATON

3 December 1924

Those in Authority

R. A. BUTLER (Pembroke)
President of the Union

'The cities are full of pride,
  Challenging each to each,'

—yet Attock Fort, in the Punjab, is the proudest one of all.
An outpost of Empire, where the Cabul and the Indus meet
—and there, in Akbar's Caravanserai, on December 9th, 1902,
first saw the light of day Richard Austen Butler of Attock
('R.A.B.').

Can anybody who knows him—and his circle of friends, let
it be said, is an extremely large one—deny on reflection that
such surroundings, and such only, were the obvious ones?

A horoscope was promptly cast and a most distinguished
man dedicated an ode to him; it is not a matter for surprise
then, that the child, born in such circumstances, soon showed
great signs of promise. He proved too much for eight succes-
sive 'ayahs' in his very first year, and his latent powers of
organisation became apparent to everybody, when at the age
of three he toured the Indian Empire.

It has now become possible to reveal the fact, without
causing political complications at Delhi, that he was the
original in the stories of 'Wee Willie Winkie' and 'Tod's
Amendment'. However, a more liberal education was considered necessary, and so, at the age of eight, he arrived at his
Preparatory School, 'The Wick', in Sussex.

There he rapidly rose to be joint Head of the school, but, ever forging on, in 1916 he was off to Marlborough.

The Classics, which now he professes to despise, occupied him for some time. We are also told that he ran about on the Downs, and it was under the influence of their solitudes that the romantic side of his character, disguised ever so carefully when you meet him, was developed.

(If you know him well, he will read you some of his poems written there.)

Suddenly he decided to take up Modern Languages, and by a veritable *tour de force* came up as a French Exhibitioner to Pembroke in 1921.

He had, it seems, spent previously some months at Deauville and Paris, moving in high financial circles, and there acquired that polished French and developed that *savoir-faire*, both so typical of him.

His progress through the various spheres of Cambridge life can only be described as meteoric. A hopeless task indeed, to attempt to enumerate the various clubs and societies of which he became President by the end of his first year. It is believed that there are only two in the 'Varsity with which he definitely has never had anything to do—the Chess Club and the Cheese-Eaters.

In the French Society he is, perhaps, at his best, though since his stay last summer at the remaining German and Austrian Courts it has been noticed that he will now only touch his cap to France.

Scotland is another country for which he cherishes a deep affection—whether because of the Scotch blood in his veins, or other reasons, is not known. The Conservative Association owes a great deal of its success to him; a Tory, if ever there was one, though *on dit* . . . with progressive leanings.

This term he is to grace yet another Presidential chair; the Union knows him well, both as a debater and an administrator. One can but wish him luck in his term of office, and say that never has the Union been in safer or more capable hands. It is his job to look after the building alterations, which will be going on, thus maintaining the tradition of his father before him.

And last, but not least: he took a 'one one' in the French Tripos last year.

Having attained all these Olympic heights one yet can safely say of him, '*Solus imperantium Vespasiarus mutatus in melius*'; in his '*mansarde pittoresquement meublée*' one is ever certain of great hospitality and cheer.

25 April 1924

Back to the Backs

E. M. FORSTER

A Canoe: River! River!

A Punt: The river never answers. What do you want?

Canoe: Anyone to play with. I am bored. Tell your boys to push you over this side.

Punt: They are all asleep, having moored me nicely. Tell yours to bring you over to me.

Canoe: They are asleep too. What is to be done?

Motor Launch: Pompha . . . Pompha . . . Pompha . . .

Canoe: Now we can manage it . . . Oh how glad I am to be with you. We'll have a real good talk and probe things. I'm not one to skim over a subject, like an Isis boat. One ought to research, surely.

Punt: Surely, and last year I went—

Falling Blossoms of the Chestnut: How d'ye do, how d'ye do, how d'ye do!

Canoe: Oh look, I must catch a blossom. I'll be back in a moment.

Punt: Canoes have no steadiness of purpose.

Blossoms of the Chestnut floating away: Farewell, farewell . . .

Canoe: I couldn't catch one.

Punt: No matter. Like yourself, they are ephemeral. (*To another punt*:) Good morrow, sister.

The Punt's Sister: Good morrow afternoon.

Punt: Sister, you have no sense of style, but being a

relative I say nothing. Grapple yourself to me. I was about to tell this canoe that last year I researched—

A Cushion: Plish! There! I knew I should fall in. How perfectly delicious.

All the Canoes: Tee hee hee, tee hee hee.

Punt Pole (*pulling the cushion out*): Lie there in the sun, and get dry, scatterbrains.

The Cushion: Pog.

The Punt: I was going to say that I have been through the lock in Nines week, and seen the races.

The Punt's Sister: Well, so have I, and so has this young gentleman. I saw him here—in fact, I'm afraid I upset him coming back.

Canoe: Have I? Did you? I can't remember anything.

The Punt (*under way at last*): I have seen the Nines and think nothing of them. They hire eight large boys and a small one to sit in them, and yet they always have some accident. Not one of them has yet reached the Backs, and just opposite me two collided with each other and were obliged to draw up to the bank at once. More haste, less speed, I say. Still one must float and let float, I suppose.

The Punt's Sister: Ah, Emily, you never spoke a truer word.

The Punt: Yes, we can't all be punts.

Double Sculler: None of us were once. Punts were unknown up here in my father's day.

Punt: Indeed! Then how does your father account for the causeway, specially constructed for punting in midstream and existing from the prehistoric period?

Double Sculler: I must be getting on to the Orchard.

Canoe: Where's that?

Double Sculler: Upper river.

Canoe: What's that?

Punt: There are three rivers—the upper, the lower, and this. Fish do say that the upper river comes out of the earth

c

and the lower goes into the sea, but nothing of the sort ever happened in my time.

CANOE: What's the sea?

DOUBLE SCULLER: The sea—barges sometimes mention it.

PUNT: How like a barge.

CANOE: And what's the earth?

MOWN GRASS FROM SCHOLARS' PIECE: My position is—where Pragmatism is so dishonest is—oh, of course, if that's your attitude!—Hall Lunch—Why shouldn't they camp in the chapel?—Hall Lunch—I like a tune I can tap to—I know what I like—I don't like what I know—Hall Lunch—The acting was so awful, so Perfectly Appalling, that I simply Scree-ee-ee-eamed. And everyone else said 'How good!'

CANOE: Oh what cultivated grass! I must gather some up and see if it won't stuff my cushion.

MOWN GRASS FLOATING AWAY: Farewell, farewell.

CANOE: I couldn't gather any. Let's make a raft instead, and all float after it down stream.

ALL THE CANOES: Oh, do let's!

PUNT: What say you, Margery? Shall we join the young people?

TRACTION ENGINE (*stopping on the bridge*): Humph!

CANOE: Who's that?

TRACTION ENGINE: Humph! What have we here? Everyone happy? This'll never do.

PUNT: It's a traction engine. It's reality, it's the hard facts of life. Oh what a lucky chance that they happened to be passing.

TRACTION ENGINE: I shall pass often enough in the future.

PUNT: A Futurist! Better and better.

TRACTION ENGINE: I see much amiss here. I see trees that must be lopped and turf that must be scarred out of recognition. I see buildings that ought never to have been built, or, if built, ought never to be put to the purposes for which they were originally intended. I shall destroy them.

PUNT: How perfectly splendid of you.

TRACTION ENGINE: I am not splendid. I come to remind you of the filth of the lower reaches and the monotony of the sea, of the winds, not heroic, that blow ships further and further from joy. I am strong but not splendid, smoky but not picturesque, clumsy, but there are no graceful little jokes to be made about me, there is nothing laughable or charming that will avert me. I am the squalor of experience. I shall come.

ALL THE BOATS: Oh how absolutely splendid! That's exactly what we want. Better than the Union or the University Sermon even. One is so in danger of getting narrow and academic. I only hope that the paddles and boat-hooks have been attentive—they are apt to wander at times.

TRACTION ENGINE: River! I cannot waste smoke over cockle shells. River! River!

PUNT: The river answers no one.

TRACTION ENGINE: He must answer me. Everyone must. It's the Universal Law. *(Silence)*

THE BOATS: Oh River, do make an exception in the Traction Engine's favour. His attitude is so splendidly interesting. *(Silence)*

TRACTION ENGINE: Humph! Well, we shall see. There's a bad time coming, and I have done my best to warn you. Humph *(going off diminuendo)* Humph, humph, humph . . .

PUNT: He's perfectly right. We ought to be clad in iron.

CANOE: I know. Let's all go and have it done. It's the only way to steer through life. Let's—*(he capsizes)*. Don't mind me. I'm just as happy upside down—happier in fact.

MORE BLOSSOMS FALLING FROM THE CHESTNUT: How d'ye do, how d'ye do, farewell, how d'ye do.

15 February 1964; but apparently written forty years earlier, and so placed here.

The Merry Widow

CECIL BEATON

As she was and as we would   As she is, alas.
always see her.

24 October 1924

Those in Authority

J. S. B. LLOYD (Magdalene)
President of the Union

At the furthermost extremity of the Wirral peninsula lies the peaceful hamlet of West Kirby. At the time our story opens, West Kirby had just increased its population by one; but the event caused little excitement among the placid Cheshire villagers. To them the twenty-eighth of July, 1904, was much what the twenty-seventh of that month had been, and indeed what the twenty-ninth proved itself to be. With so little ceremony, and such slight publicity, did John Selwyn Brooke Lloyd enter the world.

John Selwyn Brooke Lloyd was born at four o'clock in the afternoon to the tune of 'There's a Girl wanted there' from a neighbouring hurdy-gurdy. To this circumstance has been attributed much of his subsequent misogynism. The next we hear of John Selwyn Brooke Lloyd is his removal from school. The circumstances are obscure. When questioned he says little about the matter. At least it is known that he was the only boy in the school and that there were a large number of girls. At any rate, he was removed from the school.

His next attempt is at the Leas School, Hoylake. Here, apparently, he is a reformed character, for by September, 1918, we find him setting out for Fettes, with a scholarship to his credit and a clean Eton collar round his neck.

Of John Selwyn Brooke Lloyd, Fettes had five years, and he left apparently of his own free will. He was in the Rugger XV and the Hockey XI, and in a misguided fit of militarism became senior N.C.O. of the Corps. Half his time at Fettes he spent in a lordly way in the Upper Sixth. Finally he left in July, 1923, no longer with a clean Eton collar, but with some reputation, and a scholarship to Magdalene.

It is firmly believed that when he came up to the University his main ambition was to get a Rugger Blue. And for some time it seemed likely that he would succeed. He played in the Freshers' Trial his first year, then Seniors' Trials and University 'A' Fifteen matches. He soon began to wear a Hawks tie with his brown suits. But the Blue never came, and, athletically, he has had to be content with four years and a captaincy in the Magdalene Rugger side, four years in the Hockey side, while his face can be seen in the photos of last year's Magdalene Soccer XI.

At the Union John Selwyn Brooke Lloyd started slowly. In his first year he spoke only twice, in his second only six times. But in his third year he began to take himself more seriously. He rapidly composed and delivered a few soul-stirring orations, and had soon made his way to the front rank. Amid the plaudits of the multitude he became Secretary for the Lent Term, 1927, and now, immaculately dressed, and with well-tidied hair, he fills with assurance the Presidential throne.

What Cambridge has today, England wants tomorrow, and in April, 1927, John Selwyn Brooke Lloyd became Prospective Liberal Candidate for the Macclesfield Division. On arriving in the division he found to his horror that most of the electorate were young females. The Stern Misogynist was unnerved. Nor was this all. He inquired their chief employment. Making silk underwear for other young females. The Stern Misogynist fled.

His first impulse was to resign his candidature. The agent was in tears. Lord Oxford wrote to him a letter of encouragement and hope. Sir Herbert Samuel made another speech at the National Liberal Club. Mr Lloyd George meant to do something about it but forgot. The whole of the Liberal Party, with tears in their eyes, begged him to stick it. John Selwyn Brooke Lloyd stuck it.

Ah me! strange are the vagaries of Fate! Since that time the Prospective Liberal Candidate has speedily become the *beau idéal* of the Macclesfield silk operatives. By the side of many a loom a loving hand has pasted his grubby portrait. And when last he was heard of, John Selwyn Brooke Lloyd had abandoned misogynism, and had fallen desperately and horribly in love.

His spare time at Cambridge our hero devoted to taking three Triposes—Classical, Part I; History, Part II; and Law, Part II. His other recreations include playing golf, and walking over the Welsh hills composing perorations for his speeches. At golf he once played Sir John Simon, and beat him.

John Selwyn Brooke Lloyd has no vices, though he does not altogether approve of the Liberal Temperance Policy. He is a trustee of his local Wesleyan Church, but has no other conspicuous virtues. He answers to the name 'Peter'.

Hail, John Selwyn Brooke Lloyd!

14 October 1927

The Song of the Dilettantes

MICHAEL REDGRAVE

Bring me a rosewood harpsichord
   and the music to which it belongs,
or the splashy sound of Stravinsky,
   or Schubert's easier songs.

give me some violent woodcuts
   or paintings both weird and rare,
give me a wall that's stippled
   that I may hang them there.

show me a play that's Russian
   with a psycho-symbolical trend,
put me to sleep in a soft stall
   and wake me up at the end.

if Tagore or Eliot the rage is,
   then give them me, husk, rind or pith,
give me some uncut pages
   and a knife to cut them with.

bring me the bowl of the muses
   that I may skim off the cream,
art is a thing for the Arty,
   and Life a be-eautiful dream.

3 February 1928

Newly Discovered War Poems

WILLIAM EMPSON

The sappers dug through Archie yesterday.
There he was buried slap in the way of the mine.
　　　And—Oh, my God!
Scrunch.
　　　　　　Trickle, trickle, trickle.
　　　Archie used to say
　　　　　One day was like another day.
　　　His love for play on any day was gay.
　　　　He threw a many yesterdays away.
He had a better stomach, as a sapper, than I have.
　Where is this bullet?
Give it me: mud, mud, mud.
　Mud, oh, my God! Oh, my God! mud.
　　　Oh, my mud!
Ping.

2 November 1928

Major Gives Men Meat
ROUSING REVIEW ORATION

WILLIAM EMPSON

(Proud as we are to have secured this text of Major-General Plain-Bomb's address, delivered at the recent Inspection of the St Vitus School Contingent, our pleasure cannot but be tinged with regret. We had hoped to uplift our readers with the inspiring and ennobling words of a Very Exalted Person on the same occasion; he is known to have spoken highly, though guardedly, of the League of Nations and the pacific mission of our Empire; but unfortunately he was taken by many of his hearers for the Three Minutes' Silence, and our stenographers could make no headway. General Plain-Bomb, on the other hand, could be heard in Bletchley.)

Well, you young fellows, this has been a very decent show. I don't know that I have anything very serious to complain of. One thing I might say: some of these Boots didn't seem to come up to the level of the rest of the equipment. Of course I know they get dusty on the way out; can't expect you all to take taxis (Ha!); but if you'd just spat on them and wiped them up with your sleeve at the last minute it might have improved the effect, some of you. And mind you, you may think that's a small point, but you fellows, you'll have to judge your men, and it's little touches like that that'll show you the trained soldier.

Well, I shan't keep you a minute after the splendid, the altogether very fine, address you've just been listening to, but

I should just like to say a few words about the great privilege and honour which is being given to you fellows; I dare say some of you don't quite realize it yet. What you fellows have got to remember is, as soon as the next war breaks out—and mind you, it's going to come very soon, you'll find people preparing for a war some way off, but it's going to come very soon, in a few years, and what's more, it's going to be a big war; you'll find people preparing for a small war, but it's going to be a very big war, big as any we've seen, and as soon as that comes, those of you that have taken Certificate A at any rate, you'll be put straight in command of a platoon of as many as thirty men, and you'll be sent out, and you'll be allowed to gamble away the lives of those thirty men, and as soon as you've done that you'll be put in command of thirty more. Now that's a very great honour and privilege. And I'll tell you why; it's true the actual cost of a man to this country, the cost of training him for six months and throwing him into the field, that's not very much; it may not come to more than thirty pounds, all told; and you may set that against the cost of a machine-gun, which may be a hundred pounds, and when your time comes you can scatter them about the battlefield. But what you've got to remember is the question of reserves. It takes twenty years to grow a man to fight for his country, and they can turn out a machine-gun in a week. It won't be a question of money, when this country's in a life-and-death struggle; it'll be a question of manpower. You'll find you come to the end of the men long before you come to the end of the machine-guns.

So what you've got to remember is, it's not a question of money, it's a question of the vital reserves of this country. As soon as the next war breaks out, every man jack of you, those of you, as I say, that have got Certificate A, you'll be given thirty men, irreplaceable; we can't wait twenty years with the enemy at our gates and grow a new lot, thirty irreplaceable men, remember, and you can throw them away on the battlefield while you learn your job. So what I want to leave on your minds is, you're in a position of extraordinary honour and privilege, we're putting on you a great trust, a great responsibility. File out there by the right. Quietly, please!

WITH SOME HEAT

'Will you have the goodness to remove your toupet from my curry, Sir?' expostulated the major, his face suffused with suppressed indignation. Removing the malingering article from the end of his fork, I replaced it as unobtrusively as the circumstances permitted. The major ignored my apology. 'Good Gad, Sir, and to think that I once tasted curry.' I registered adequate sympathy and brushed away a shred of rice, which was still adhering to my forelock. The major looked over and through me simultaneously as he continued:

'You people that haven't been to India are content with any damned anaemic mess they like to give you. We would have put the cooks in C.B., back in the Punjab, if they'd served up this cat's food. Why, Colonel Grouch of the 69th ("Sandy Grouch") used to say that curry that didn't take the skin off the tip of the tongue was only fit for the latrines! Burn your guts, that's what it ought to do if you've got any.' I winced and dropped my left eye unwittingly into a salt-cellar; the major swept both to the ground. 'By Heavens, Sir, what do you think your guts are for. When we took Mysore we'd not eaten for five days. What did we eat? Charcoal biscuits? No! Damned effeminate chicken? No! CURRY! HOT . . . AS . . . HELL. Three men died of internal combustion. You should have seen the Begums flipping it up: I myself, as a matter of fact, sweated through nine dungarees. Good Gad . . .' Here the major was seized with a devastating spasm and I observed him surreptitiously remove a Pepper-corn from his mouth and gulp down two tumblers full of water. It was during that interval that I extricated my ear-trumpet from the mashed potatoes.   *2 November 1928*

A Little Bit about Christmas

MICHAEL REDGRAVE

It was just a week ago that the editor asked me to write a little bit about Christmas. I just looked at him and said what. He seemed to think I hadn't heard and repeated would I write a little bit about Christmas. Then he said something about turning it out. As if I were a prize Buff-Warpington. Or a cow. I looked at him in a marked way for some time and said with some intensity anything else? Yes he said casual like you might turn out a limerick or two or a funny poem. I left him at that for I was near tears. Between you and me the Editor has no line of thought. That's what's wrong with this paper. No line of thought. None at all. Now look at a paper like the *Review*. Now that has got a line of thought. The purest and sweetest weekly. I mean to say the *Review* doesn't have any nonsense about little bits about Christmas. If the editor of the *Review* were to ask me to write a little bit about Christmas I should laugh in his face. Run about the streets and grin like a dog. I mean to say it's all over with Christmas stories. *Vieux jeu*, that's what they are. I reckon if forty or so Christmas numbers of the *Granta* haven't said all there is in the way of little bits about Christmas, it's not for me to start digging skeletons out of the cupboard.

Besides I am not the sort of man to write a thing like that. I'm a poet. Now I said to the Editor now old man if you want a poem I'm the man, I'll write you a poem, and a jolly good poem it'll be. He didn't even look at me as he muttered it had damn well better be. Hang it all I said, but stopped. I know when to let well alone. If a man hasn't got a line of thought it seems to me no good arguing about it at all. So I just looked at him and went. Now what I ought to be doing— Well well one ought to have a stab at it. 'O look said little Nancy as she *jumped* out of bed and flung open the window, look Nurse the ground is *covered* with snow. . . .'

No, it's useless. I can't write little bits about Christmas. I haven't got it in me. Now I'm not Milton. Milton just reeled out bits about Christmas when he was up here. He wrote the *Nativity Ode* when he was an undergraduate, did you know? But he probably had some paper with a line of thought to do it for. I shall just go to the Editor and tell him what I think. Perhaps he can write a little bit about Christmas. Anyway there must be somebody who can write a little bit about Christmas. Damn it all man only a wee little bit. About Christmas? Yeah! about Christmas.

30 November 1928

The Meaning of Meaning

ALISTAIR COOK

I. A. RICHARDS

If this young man expresses himself
In terms too deep for me,
Why what a most particularly deep young man
This deep young man must be.

8 February 1929

Verandah, a Biography

VIRGINIA WOOLF

(MICHAEL REDGRAVE)

PREFACE

Of the many illustrious names which I could quote as collaborators in this book I will only mention a few, chosen quite at random. To Mrs Gordon I am indebted for the details of Cambridge Life during the Caroline period, to Mr Julian Bell for my knowledge of Botany, Zoology and Cosmology, to Mr Wittgenstein for my high moral attitude, to Mr Anthony Blunt for a Pre-Raphaelite service, and to the Almighty for my disregard of Time, Space and Sexual Continuity.

CHAPTER IV

VERANDAH, leaning elegantly on the parapet of a bridge, a garland in stone newly laced across the Cam, was wondering, idly enough, when last it was that he had changed his sex. It was the sight of the river craft that prompted this reflection, for the stream was patterned with slowly moving boats, of every shape, colour and size, some with prows carven into the forms of birds (especially of swans and other water-fowl), some with bright silks filleting the tresses of the waves with floating ribbons, some undecorated save for the vigorous lines of a young man's body or the brocaded dress and white neck of a girl, who lay among deep pillows on the water like a slender, gauze-skirted dragonfly in the cup of a lily. Life, thought Verandah, seems a matter of position: either one is decorative upright on the poop, or prostrate in the bows. So often had he done both that it had ceased to be amusing to speculate about either. To one who was uncertain of what turn his sexual arrangements might take at any minute, this languishment of river transport held little excitement.

In the time of the Virgin Queen, Verandah, as royal ambassador in a tunic of flowered silk, had entertained a foreign visitor, the Princess of Granada, in a pleasure dinghy on the Cam. He had been telling the princess, a woman of rich southern beauty but a lamentably nordic turn of wit, about his great picture of a primrose, long tended and yet unfinished, when to his horror he perceived (for who can foretell and forestall these usually untimely occurrences?) that his old trick was reasserting itself, and before he knew where he was he had changed into a woman before the astonished eyes of the unhappy lady, who thereupon fell, overcome with chagrin and amazement, into the water and was drowned. It was in memory of this unfortunate Princess of Granada, the historians tell us, that the Cam river became known by the lugubrious pseudonym of Granta.

On the next day he would in all probability have received his sixth degree and commenced a study of British flora and dates of kings, when, with a profusion and unexpectedness that have been found wanting in our climate ever since, began the Great Heat.

The Great Heat, the astrologers tell us, was irrefutably due to an unexampled and quite extraordinary period of relative proximity between sun and earth. Certainly the sun seemed nearer. The leaves turned rapidly through several shades and fell to the ground. To balance this premature denudation a heavy and prolific undergrowth sprang up—especially in the Fens around Cambridge, and wherever there was water the vegetation became dense and of tropical behaviour, purpling the air with wild fruits and flowers. Humming birds and gay parrakeets threaded the branches with their jewelled wings and shrill cries, and perched voluptuously on the branches of gaudy and obscene creepers, while in the river a rumour spread of a ravaging crocodile, which, although but of small size, was believed to have crossed from Chile in the Gulf Stream. An ancient don of King's College was crossing the waving lawns of tall tropical ferns when he was bitten by a rattlesnake of considerable venom. Fewer clothes were worn, though, of course, not markedly so. A dean of some girth, in the heat of the moment, forgot to clothe himself in anything but a surplice, but this ruse was discovered and caused much conjecture and scandal in the Senate.

We learn from books that the brown peoples under southern skies and Eskimo snowhouse dwellings in the north lead a life far different from ours, and, as might be expected, this atmospheric extreme produced remarkable and not always publishable effects in the lives of our ancestors. Clothing was moderated. Puberty had to be revised. Verandah himself had the greatest difficulty in remaining alive, definitely. No sooner had he issued forth in silk breeches and a boating garb than he was forced to hurry back and don a dress of taffeta or bombazine. No caterpillar underwent more changes of life and thought in its remarkable metamorphoses. As for his picture of the primrose, it was temporarily discontinued, for primroses had ceased to be. As a last expedient Verandah, abandoned by art and life, was forced to go to bed, where, like a doubting chrysalis, he or she shall now be left.

CHAPTER V

It was in the 'sixties of the last century when Verandah woke one morning to find herself the soul-mate of a leading Pre-Raphaelite. Her picture of the primrose, to comply with the persuasion of the period, had to be painted again with a background of madonna lilies, and was greatly admired. . . . All her friends faded away, like the centuries, unnoticed. . .

She would have liked to bury her Pre-Raphaelite consort in Pisa, but when she looked for him one day, he was nowhere to be found, and she discovered herself sitting at the paradoxical feet of the 'nineties, with dear Oscar making epigrams about her art, and Max caricatures of her person and soul. . . .

The other day Verandah was seen in Piccadilly. The present mode of dress, being delightfully ambiguous, was standing her in good stead, and for the first time for many years she had ceased to worry about her figure. The picture of the primrose was hung on the line in this season's academy, and was bought for the long expectant nation, after its creator had been awarded the Nobel prize, a Travelling Scholarship in Arts and Crafts, an enamelled plaque in Gordon Square, and the Royal Botanical Society's Gold Medal.

7 June 1929

Mediaeval Expert

Professor Coulton

31 January 1934

The Nazi Movement and the Universities
by a Special Correspondent
(J. J. BRONOWSKI)

The National Socialist revolution in Germany is most deeply founded, has its most bigoted and best organised support in the German universities. To anyone familiar only with English universities and perhaps the *Sorbonne*, this is a surprising fact. But it is not surprising to anyone who understands the part of the Spanish universities in the recent revolution in Spain, or who reads the journals of the Polish or Hungarian universities, or who remembers how substantially the suppressed Russian revolution of 1905 drew upon the universities. I have hitherto regretted that English universities did not share, not the politics but the capacity for enthusiasm of those universities. Having seen the rise in Germany of what is so considerably a university movement, I temper my regret.

Germany has not many universities proper; but it has a host of *Handelschochschulen*, *Technische Hochschulen* and others, which I have classed together as universities and as forming—with the *Abitur*-forms of the *Gymnasien* and *Realgymnasien*—a mainstay of active National Socialism. The staff of these institutions is almost entirely royalist and rabidly nationalist. Anyone who has read accounts of the expulsion of the German Jews from the legal and medical professions may have wondered why no similar drive was being made against Jews in university and school appointments. But no such drive was necessary; these appointments have been virtually closed to Jews, Socialists, and indeed any but right-minded nationalists for many years. As well begin a drive against non-nationalist colonels. This nationalist solidarity of teachers and lecturers has had a profound effect upon the generation which has grown up since the war, as it did upon the generation which went into the war. (I was at school in Germany during the war, and remember seeing the sixth form learning to throw hand-grenades, in school hours.) The effect has not been one merely of nationalism. It has been also a morbid reverence for the donnish and faded elegance of the pre-war court—and for its equally donnish authority. And it has been a credulity, even a demand, for the academic doctrinairism of Hitler's Aryan or *Blutsgefühl* twaddle. These now govern Germany.

This academic ascendency in the Nazi movement is to be remarked, above all, in its passionate provincialism. Germany at her entry into the war was a great power. The Versailles treaty tried clumsily to depose her; but she has since been deposed much more effectively by her own teachers and professors. The treaty was unjust, and it allowed the universities to canalise into a sense of national injustice that petty fury of impotence which comes with academic ageing. In this way German post-war patriotism was pitched upon that shrill and querulous note which had only occasionally been heard there before the war, but which had been the prerogative of the Balkan states and of the oppressed Poles, Czechs, Roumanians and Bosnians. This is the note of the nationalism of Hitler— himself a Czech. It is the smallholder's nationalism, posturing tragically that every man's hand is against him, inventing spectre after spectre—finance, Jews, Socialism, Jazz, modern art—because it exists only in opposition. It is a husk of personality, it has no core of self-knowledge or self-possession, and like its professors there is nothing it fears more than to be left alone face to face with itself.

This shrill and academic provincialism is responsible for the savagery of the Nazi movement. No one could have believed that the brutal sadism to which for a moment it gave rein had survived the Boxer rising and Kishinieff, or could take place west of Roumania. Yet the nationalist German was apparently content to assert his Teutonism by imitating the most backward of the Slav countries on the borders of Asia. Perhaps no other answer is needed to Hitler's Aryan cry than this, that provincialism and persecution-mania bite deeper than blood. And National Socialism pictures itself as persecuted, not only by the political world but by art, science and philosophy. The treatment of Professor Einstein may be taken as typical. The National Socialist government now claims that Professor Einstein made anti-German statements abroad. But anyone who remembers the behaviour of the nationalists some years ago, when the city of Berlin offered to present him with a house, can hardly respect the claim. Professor Einstein is certainly the greatest scientist of some generations: the rabid provincialism which, discounting his achievement, sees only the slight to its own petty administration stands self-accused. With Professor Einstein suffer some thousands of intellectuals of world reputation. In the meantime, the Nazi government is founding a special order for true nationalist artists who, in its opinion, are distinguished. No doubt the patron saint will be Wagner; and all that is characterless and third-rate in art will have a stronghold in the Balkan state which once was Germany.

For this we must not disguise from ourselves: National Socialism has come to Germany for a long time. That recognition will no doubt alter the present protesting tone of European politicians very quickly. It cannot alter sane opinion of this German abdication from the state of a great power. I have referred to the politics of Polish and Hungarian university journals. Reading one of these recently, *La Tribune des Jeunes*, I was appalled by its blind and petty anti-German propaganda. Now National Socialism has reduced Germany to

the status of Poland and Hungary, catspaws of European
politics which live only in their hatred of the greater and
more durable. The change, I have suggested, marks the
ascendancy of all that is worst in academicism and university
dogmatism. With it learning and education die, and bigotry
stalks the land.

19 April 1933

Hitlerism

J. J. BRONOWSKI

By the time this appears, the Union will have expressed, in words perhaps unnecessarily crude, its opinion of German National Socialism. To those interested only in the day to day politics of the fall of the dollar and the Russian embargo, this University interest in a month-old revolution in Germany may appear belated. On the contrary, we believe this interest to be salutary and opportune. For we believe, first, that the issues of the Nazi revolution are issues which vitally concern the Universities. And, second, we believe that only now has come the time to see these issues in themselves, out of the context of cruelty and outrage which Herr Hitler's storm-troops created for them.

Our correspondent last week indicated how considerably National Socialism is a University movement. It is a movement motivated by the bigoted provincialism of German University professors. But more than this, it is a movement for unemployed graduates and Public School boys. To this extent it is a movement created by the Versailles Treaty: a movement to employ the enforced leisure of those who have been deprived, for example by the annexation of the German Colonies, of the opportunity to bully natives in the Eastern services. Such a movement arises in any defeated state. It might have arisen in England, had the Allies not won the Pyrrhic victory of the War. But it has been aggravated in Germany by the frightening spread of University education.

Every School and University produces a proportion of what, on the most charitable view, can only be called educated illiterates. In England their number, if not their proportion, is limited by the smallness of the Public Schools and the Universities; and by the fact that the unemployment problem in the middle classes has not here become sufficiently acute to demand an exorbitant standard of technical education from candidates for employment. But Germany is peopled with such educated illiterates; with men who can read but hate literature, who can experiment but hate science, with men who speak English and French but who hate England and France. They constitute the Nazi movement, and indeed the movement is their protest against the education which has been imposed upon them. They regard this education as alien —a word for which the German synonym now is apparently 'Jewish'. But their protest is not against Jewish or Socialist cultures, which do not exist. Their protest is against European culture. That is why their action, and the conditions of education which created it, are of vivid and permanent interest to the Universities. That is why the burning of the books on May 10 is a flame still licking up from the gutted library of Constantinople.

In thus stating our view of the Nazi movement, we can hardly be accused of subscribing to what Herr Hitler calls 'the atrocity campaign'. Elsewhere this week we publish an article, not defending National Socialism, but asking for its more tolerant examination. The two main points of this article are those also of the various statements made by the German Government: that German youth has been forced by post-war events into its present attitude, and that the agitation against Nazi excesses obscures the issues and implications of the movement. To the first point, which indeed we have laboured, there is an obvious reply. German youth has had many provocations in the past fifteen years for behaving outrageously. But the justification of the responsible movement lies not in the past but in the future: not in what it has suffered but in what it undertakes. Nothing that the Nazi Government has yet undertaken, nothing that it proposes, shows it to be inspired by any but the spirit of provincialism which our correspondent last week deplored, and the spirit of ignorance which we deplore. This then is our answer to the second point. We have tried to examine the principles and ambitions of National Socialism. In so far as we have succeeded, we have found them mediaeval and bigoted, shrill with professorial impotence and with undergraduate aimlessness. It is these principles which we ask the University to ponder; and to us they are more alarming than the most wilful of Nazi persecutions.

26 April 1933

Poems and Drawings

STEVIE SMITH

Henry Wilberforce as a child
Was much addicted to the pleasures of the wild;
He observed Nature, saw, remembered,
And was by a natural lion dismembered.

MARRIAGE I THINK

Marriage I think
For women
Is the best of opiates.
It kills the thoughts
That think about the thoughts,
It is the best of opiates.
So said Maria.
But too long in solitude she'd dwelt,
And too long her thoughts had felt
Their strength. So when the man drew near,
Out popped her thoughts and covered him with fear.
Poor Maria!
Better that she had kept her thoughts on a chain,
For now she's alone again and all in pain;
She sighs for the man that went and the thoughts that
    stay
To trouble her dreams by night and her dreams by day.

9 *June 1937*

LULU

I do not care for Nature,
    She does not care for me;
You can be alone with a person,
    You can't be alone with a tree.

Two Drawings

RONALD SEARLE

Not Angels but Engels

30 November 1938

'When I roped those steers back home in Colorado'

8 March 1939

John Cornford, 1915–1936

On December 28th, John Cornford, scholar of Trinity College, Cambridge, Commander of the English Group in the first International Brigade, and later of an infantry group in the English Battalion, was killed at the head of his men on the Cordova front. It was not until one month later that confirmation of his death reached England from Spain.

To the many who knew him this is a bitter loss. To the Socialists of this University he was from the time he came up a beloved leader, whose genius for organisation and whose tremendous energy arose out of his devotion to others, and his deep understanding of their problems. It was these qualities which made him the deepest experience of our lives. We shall never forget him.

He came up to Cambridge after a year at the London School of Economics, where he had joined the Communist Party. From the beginning he was one of the leaders of the Communist group, and devoted himself to building up the Socialist Movement in the University. The transformation of the University Socialist Society from a small organisation preoccupied with theoretical problems into the movement which in his last year sent two hundred students to work for the Labour Candidate during the whole of the General Election campaign, was largely the result of his leadership and example. Not only was he mainly responsible for the achievement of unity amongst the left-wing parties of Cambridge University, but it was largely due to him that the University Labour Federation, of which he was a Vice-President, became nationally the one organisation in which unity between Communists and Socialists exists. At the same time he wrote articles on Communism in *Christianity and the Social Revolution* and *New Minds for Old*, and he was actively associated with the editorship of *Student Vanguard* and the pamphlet *British Armaments and World Peace*.

In his last year he joined the Union and spoke frequently there. His sincerity and determination earned him respect on all sides; within a term he was elected a member of the committee, and he was re-elected in the following term.

His academic career was outstanding. He won an Open Major Scholarship at Trinity College from Stowe School before he was seventeen. After two terms at the London School of Economics he came up to Cambridge in October, 1933. He read History, obtaining a First in Part I and a starred First in Part II. On graduating he was awarded the Earl of Derby Research Scholarship in History. He had begun research work on the period of early capitalism in Britain, when the Spanish rebellion began.

As soon as it became evident that Italy was sending warplanes to Franco, the issues at stake in the Spanish rebellion, and its importance, became clear. Long before anyone else, John Cornford realized the importance of volunteer work in Spain; as always, he himself carried out his own decisions. He resigned his scholarship and left immediately for the Spanish frontier.

In early August he arrived in Barcelona and joined a column of the Spanish militiamen, leaving for the Aragon front. That was his baptism of fire. But seeing the contrast between the military efficiency of the rebel army and the unpreparedness of the people for war, he realized that only a great effort on the part of the democracies of the world could save democracy in Spain. With this message he returned to England in late September to form a British Section of the Spanish People's Army. Three weeks later he left with seven others for Albacete. Among them was another student from Cambridge, who returned, wounded, to England on January 29th. He writes of the months when they were comrades in arms :

'We left for Albacete in early October and there met fourteen other English, and the twenty-one of us became "les Anglais" in the French Battalion of the First International Brigade. There John was our political delegate, agitating in bad but forceful French for our recognition as an English group, guiding our own stormy meetings out of the disputes that arose among the twenty-one isolated Englishmen to just decisions. From the military command of our group, to which we wished to elect him, he stood down in favour of older and more experienced soldiers.

'From the peaceful town a twenty-four hours' lorry-ride took us to University City, barring the path of Franco's "triumphal entry" into Madrid. There we stayed for a costly four weeks that reduced our numbers by half, and through those weeks John's cheerfulness, his coolness under fire, and his power of command gave others his own courage. Some memories of him in those days come to my mind now, memories of John taking command of two Lewis gun crews in a dispersal under barrage fire, of John, withdrawn to rest positions after a costly advance, volunteering as an extra stretcher-bearer for the front line, John wounded in the head by a shell that came into our front line room in the University coming back to his post after twenty-four hours in hospital.

'In our week's rest that followed the November attack on Madrid, the thirteen of us who were left reorganised ourselves. Our commander had been killed, his successor wished to resign, and John was unanimously elected to fill his place. It was under him that we went in mid-December up to Boadilla del Monte to face the hardest attack of all. There under his command we moved back slowly on one sunny morning, covering the battalion's retreat, while John under fire went from one gun to the other directing operations. Some days later, lying wounded in a Madrid hospital, I was told that in the opinion of the battalion commander, the British section had distinguished itself above all others on that day.

'In that hospital two days later I saw him for the last time. He was off with five survivors of our English group to join the recently formed English battalion. His head wound was giving him trouble, but he was as cheerful as I have ever seen him. Sometime later, in a hospital at the base, I met an Englishman from John's section, wounded on the Cordova front, who told me of John's death.'

He was killed the day after his twenty-first birthday.

3 February 1937

Part Two

1945 – 1966

Editors' Note

Granta's career since the war has been an extremely varied one, but its main problem has always been the same, namely that of continuing to be heard in a Cambridge whose tastes and modes of life have been changing decade by decade, if not year by year. In the middle 'forties it was a sorry affair, badly designed, and packed with heavy and rather desperate university humour. In the late 'forties, under the guidance of Jonathan Routh and the Schaffer brothers, came the necessary reaction to such parochialism. The products of this time were professional indeed. A favourite ploy was to devote a whole issue to a take-off of a national magazine, not only parodying its content, but also copying its whole typographical format. Although this was a step in the right direction, and these issues must have been considerably more amusing and stimulating than the old Cambridge japes, yet there was a danger of carrying it too far. *Granta* after all was a Cambridge magazine, and would lose its point if it drifted too far away from the life of the university. In the early 'fifties one can see the attempt being made to reintegrate the magazine in this way. However, reintegration also meant change, for much of the talent of this time was of a serious rather than a frivolous or satiric nature, perhaps reflecting a similar change in the atmosphere of the university. *Granta*, then, to be a university magazine had to reflect this new seriousness. However, the old tradition of wit and irreverence was too strong to be given up entirely, so the new formula for the magazine became the combination of these two elements. This situation, instigated by Victor Sandelson in 1952, was nourished by Mark Boxer (whose literary adviser was Thom Gunn), and became the accepted condition under which the magazine worked. There ensued one of *Granta*'s most fruitful periods. Good work of all sorts, poetry, prose, criticism, and satire, all jostle for the reader's attention. Among those writing for the magazine at this time were Ronald Bryden, John Coleman, Thom Gunn, Nicholas Tomalin, Karl Miller, Leslie Bricusse, and Neal Ascherson. Among those soon to arrive were Michael Frayn, Jonathan Miller, Ted Hughes, and Sylvia Plath.

It is this combination of levity and seriousness that has remained the framework of *Granta* up to this day. However, no period is as rich in both fields as that just described. In the later 'fifties there are individual successes of all sorts, but the total picture is less impressive. Most of the Cambridge satirists later to make big names for themselves contributed to the magazine, but it never became wholly devoted to their work. David Frost became editor in 1960, but he, like all his predecessors, was eager to promote the serious side of the magazine as well as its humour. Perhaps the most consistent move of the last few years has been that towards wider cultural interest. *Granta*'s characteristic role in the 'sixties has been as an avant-garde arts magazine reflecting, and to a certain extent creating, the taste of its audience. It has become more excitable, and in some ways more naïve, no doubt reflecting the attitudes of its younger post-national service editors. However, there is something extremely engaging in these yearly attempts by each editorial board to reassess and reinvigorate the culture around them. It is done with a serious purpose, but with an elegance and a professionalism that is *Granta*'s own and unique among student magazines.

A few words should be said about this selection. There are three pieces included that illustrate some of the ways in which different writers have tried to grasp and express the nature of the university. The first two, by Eric Hobsbawm and Ronald Bryden, are vivid personal accounts. The third, by Pat Rogers, a young don in Sidney, introduces some of the important new problems that face Cambridge today, particularly its relations to the new universities, and the move for reform of teacher–pupil relationships.

In the selection of other prose articles, the intention has been partly to point to the diversity of material that has appeared in the magazine. In the early 'fifties, series of articles were in favour, of which the most striking were the 'One Man's Week' pieces. *Granta* has also published a wealth of good stories, of which we have only been able to include one. Other storytellers have included Brian Glanville, David Gillies, Peter Green, and Rima Allamuddin. The article on E. M. Forster must be allowed to stand for acres of criticism of all sorts into which *Granta* writers have poured their energies. The humour may be left to speak for itself. As for the poetry it is perhaps worth noticing that there has never been anything that might be called a *Granta* school of poets. The policy of the magazine has always been to print 'the best Cambridge writing', and in poetry, as in all else, this often takes startlingly diverse forms.

Modern Times

JONATHAN ROUTH

Socio-dramatic theatres are springing up all over industrial Gloucestershire, writes my Tyneside correspondent.

It took me a long time to find out the whys and wherefores of this cult, he says. A very long time. Six out of seven directors of one pylon factory I visited knew they had a socio-dramatist on the premises, but excused themselves before I could ask why. The seventh director was more approachable. 'When a man writes in to us applying for a job at £6,000 a year we don't care whether he's a socio-dramatist or a . . . a . . . nuisance administrator,' he explained before he too excused himself.

Leaving the shed I came out into the open and found myself standing in the path of four overalled labourers staggering beneath the weight of a vast canvas and framework backcloth representing the interior of a machine shop (surely that very same machine shop I had just left?). 'Here, let me give you fellows a hand,' I suggested. 'You a member?' one from among them asked. 'Of what?' I asked, catching on with more than usual quickness. 'Union,' replied the fellow—'can't carry scenery unless you are.' I had to admit I wasn't. 'Ah, well,' he said, 'I dare say we'll manage. Why don't you go see Miss Prosser?'

Miss Prosser, I found, knew all about socio-dramatism, and she told me. 'You see,' she explained, 'when there's a row in the works, when some worker punches some bloody-minded foreman on the nose, that's where the socio-dramatist comes in. One of his observers—we have three to each shed here— reports the incident to him. He sends one of his deputies to the shed to get hold of the two contestants in the quarrel. Then he takes them to the research room where the research workers take down their case histories. Their notes are passed on to the socio-dramatic playwright and he writes them up— in play-form of course. Then it's up to the producers and the actors. They rehearse it and within twenty-four hours the worker and the foreman are sitting in the socio-dramatic theatre and watching the play. It's all terribly psychological: the play shows the two disputants exactly why they disputed and at the end they shake hands with each other, vow eternal comradeship and go back to their work. Of course, it wasn't always so simple as that. Originally the disputants themselves were made to re-enact their quarrel, but we found this had certain disadvantages, and it meant one of us had to do a big strong man to sort of separate them. Now the disputants are in the role of socio-dramatic critics while the actors take their parts on the stage; naturally the climax comes in the third act—what you might call the fight scene—and we're always very careful to reproduce the exact background—I think you saw one just being taken in.'

'I see,' I said, 'and the socio-dramatist organises all this?' 'Well, sort of,' she answered—'he gets £6,000 a year, you know.'

Punctopapyrists (bus ticket collectors to you) will be pleased to hear of a new issue that has just been released in the Protochakaratti province of Hyderabad. This ticket, available in 6, 7, and 9 anna denominations, is valid for journeys between the villages of Gaylore, Badhol, and Sanskin. Present prices range between 2d. and 5d. for the unpunched 8 anna ticket, and up to £3 10s. od. for the rare underprinted reverse-coupled 9 anna variation.

The ticket was designed by Mr George Fenning of Birmingham, who is doing a grand job helping Britain's export drive. Last year his work alone reduced the dollar gap from $5,125,763,612 to $5,125,763,523, a rare achievement.

The latest British designed tickets are causing a sensation in New York where as many as 160,132 a week are being sold by officers of the British Council. 'It's their soft homespun quality we go for,' said one leading New York buyer just before being fined £5,000 by Southampton customs men. 'Quality tells,' declared another American business man, adding, 'America wants bus tickets that last.' And figures show that the tastier, more economical, and more easily man-oeuvrable British models are gaining the favour of world markets.

But British manufacturers complain that controls are menacing the prospects of this exportable commodity.

James Quill, popular Editor-in-Chief of a large North Country ticket factory, complained last week, 'The Ministries simply won't allow us the variety. Before the war, I edited more than three thousand types of tickets a year, sometimes with as many as fifty thousand place names to check and re-write. Now we are not allowed to import more than one thousand place names a month, of which at least 75% must be British.'

However, with hopes of larger supplies of punch-holes and greater serial numbers on the horizon, it is hoped that the British ticket industry may soon set new world records.

Something's got to be done about Britain's soap situation. Just read the advertisements for even three different brands out of the 200 on the English market:

'Two out of every two persons use MILK Soap.'

'Nine out of every ten cleanies use SILK Soap.'

'Six persons use BILK Soap' (maybe this costs too much, or perhaps it's only just come on the market).

And so on: $7\frac{1}{2}$ out of every 8 sandwich executives, 16 punctuation designers out of every 8 camp fire followers—they all use soap.

Adding it all up, it works out that approximately 136 out of every 5 persons uses it, therefore one person has in his possession at one time 65 pieces of soap.

This is sheer extravagance. Besides, 65 pieces of soap on a basin make a wash room look so untidy.

What are you going to do with the stuff?

You can't eat it, unless of course, when you cook it, you let it boil away to nothing at all. There seem to be several possible solutions:

1. Rewrite *Macbeth* to include a bar of soap. I'm not quite sure how this would help matters but I think it has something to do with charades.

2. Make holes in a bar of soap—round holes, square holes, funny holes. Have a few friends round in the evening and ask them to compete with one another in seeing who can make the funniest hole, using only his fingers and teeth as tools.

3. Walk into a pub, hand everyone a piece of soap and leave quickly.

4. Carve the bars out so that they fit over your nephew's ears. Thus putting an end to aunts who ask him whether he used soap behind his ears this morning.

Results of the latest nation-wide investigation into the polling habits of Englishmen have given pollsters their biggest headache since they set up in business. The purpose of the enquiry was to discover whether or not in the public's opinion polls are or are not a Good Thing. Questions asked and replies given to the Panel of Sporting Pollsters were as follows.

1. *What sort of polls do you like taking part in?* Three ex-burghers of Calais said it depended how much they got out of it, and the remainder said: don't know; it varies; it depends

what sort of poll you mean, doesn't it; ah, that'd be telling; and Jim'll be home in ten minutes and he'll know.

2. *Do you consider the poll to be an accurate way of obtaining information?* The three ex-burghers of Calais said it depended how much they got out of it, and then after a short pause, Yes. The remainder said: 'Take a poll about war with Russia, I mean. Maybe you ask a thousand people and they'll all say Yes, No, and Don't Know. Doesn't prove anything, though, do it? After all, if you're not going to ask everybody why not ask the M.P.s who are entitled to speak for others. No, I don't think you can.'

3. *What is your idea of a perfect poll?* Nearly half said walking or some other fairly strenuous exercise. One in four said Wrestling in the Hills, and an elderly spinster of High Holborn broke down and confessed: 'Last year I sat out in my pretty garden and watched the lilies, then I went indoors and had a cup of char.' A man was later detained in Piccadilly.

4. *What is the alternative to a Poll?* Three out of four said: Golly, they didn't know there was one, and the rest said 'Pack some old virgin up to the top of Ben Nevis and use her as a good old-fashioned oracle.'

So now you see why the headache. If the sporting pollsters are to be faithful to their concepts they must agree with the public that polls are inaccurate and a waste of time. But that's going to put them all out of jobs. Commented ace-pollster Ellery Boffin: 'I don't know, really I don't know.' Perhaps here lies a clue to the future activities of pollsters.

Christmas edition, 1949

In Defence of the 'Thirties

ERIC HOBSBAWM

Now that the more fashionable Cambridge figures discuss the merits of Edwardian clothes, and *Varsity* describes the political opinions of last year's firsts as 'vaguely conservative', it is time to strike a lonely blow for the Nineteen Thirties. In normal times this would be quite unnecessary. At weekends it would be barely possible to turn a stone without dislodging some visiting graduate anxious to inform his juniors how golden the age was fifteen years ago. The situation would be very similar to that of Harriette Wilson, the well-known Regency courtesan, whose first official lover, the Earl of Craven, had campaigned in the West Indies. Readers of *Granta* will doubtless recall the episode :

'I resided on the Marine Parade, at Brighton; and I remember that Lord Craven used to draw cocoa trees, and his fellows, as he called them, on the best vellum paper for my amusement. Here stood the enemy, he would say; and here, my love, are my fellows; there the cocoa trees, etc. It was, in fact, a dead bore.'

We of the Nineteen Thirties have not, of course, given over boring you. That would be against human nature. Most of us —at any rate the frighteningly large number which gets into print—specialise in the tedium of telling you how mistaken we were about politics. There are times when the noise of breast-beating and intellectual self-analysis sounds like a drum and fife band. In this country we have fortunately not yet got

to the point of hiring advertising space in the public press to
explain (a) what dreamy fools we were to give money to
Republican Spain and (b) why it is morally right to give Con-
gressional Committees the names of our friends who were
with us in the Communist Party. This may for the moment be
left to members of the American entertainments profession.
On the other hand the absence of a Senator McCarthy enables
us to claim that our confessions of guilt and remorse are
genuinely spontaneous.

One hesitates to point out that there is no need for all these
souls to be bared, because to do so sounds nostalgic, and
therefore quite uncharacteristic of the Thirties. We were
distinctly unsentimental about the past, though perhaps not
about the future. Unlike French intellectuals today, we did
not construct a pastoral world of hansom cabs, gentlemen in
moustaches and cocottes and label it '1900'; unlike English
ones, we did not evoke Victorian moral strength. We had
enough moral fervour to give it away gratis in front of Mill
Lane lecture rooms and up and down K.P., and we disapproved
of *poules de luxe* (though of course there were few of them
about in Cambridge). Few of us would have preferred to be
born in our grandparents' or great-grandparents' time; or
sympathised with those older citizens who complained that
someone had taken the silver spoons out of their mouths since
birth. Hence even the most passionate and unregenerate survivors of the Thirties are in honour bound not to senti-
mentalise them either; a fairly easy task, since there is
obviously no going back to them. The mind creaks under the
strain of imagining Mr Attlee returning to visit the Clem
Attlee Company of the 15th International Brigade, Mr John
Strachey once again instructing us in revolutionary Marxism,
and Stephen Spender advancing leftwards under the red banner
with Lehmann. For better or worse the orange patches of the
Left Book Club choices have vanished from the bookcases.
The only Marxism which has survived among the Cambridge

masses (from those days) is that of Groucho, Harpo and Chico, whose conquest of Cambridge coincided roughly with the publication of the Selected Works of Lenin. (One notes with interest that in Oxford they never became public institutions. Certainly nobody has ever set 'De Fratribus Marx' as the subject for a university latin prize essay, as happened here in, I think, 1938.)

But if there won't be another generation quite like ours (and to judge by some of its products, that may not be a bad thing), there is no reason why there should not once again be a political era in Cambridge; that is to say an era of progressive politics. There have been several such periods in Cambridge history—for instance the Radical age of the 1820s and 1830s, and the mixed socialist-rebel age which overlapped the first world war. Ours, of course, was easily the most political of all. I do not suppose there was ever anything to compare with that pre-war year when the President of the Union, the editor of *Granta* and the President of the A.D.C. were all in the Communist Party while something like 20 per cent. of all undergraduates belonged to C.U.S.C. and £1,000 could be collected in one week for Spain. Still, in their day Tennyson (who was for International Brigades in Spain) and Rupert Brooke must have behaved quite like our lot. There is much to be said for such political periods. For one thing, there is plenty to be changed in the world and we ought therefore to change it. For another, political undergraduates, like pike in a fish-pond, liven up universities, and especially their senior members, for it is a well-known fact that dons are on the whole much more influenced by undergraduates than the other way round. 'Politics' is naturally to be understood as meaning left-wing politics, for the history of right-wing student movements, of which there have been plenty, has been one of muscular rather than intellectual activities. This, then, is a plea for more politics in undergraduate life. However, as ours was the political generation *par excellence*, we may as well serve as a general illustration of how a set-up of that kind works.

Here it may be necessary to correct the two impressions which an incautious reading of the literature suggests: that life was both tedious and sinister. This is not the way it struck us. It is only in the heads of those who have read too much Koestler that life was lived against a background of impending doom, where little could be heard except the shrill whistles of intellectual n.c.o.s drilling their squads along the party line, the tramping of poster-parades on Market Hill and the sinister rustling of Natural Sciences Part II men being instructed in the use of secret codes. Indeed, life was by and large about as uneventful as it usually is; and is bound to be. Our period of history has a good deal more boy-scout and cloak-and-dagger activities in it than the Victorian and Edwardian one—at any rate in middle-class European countries—but not quite so much as one is inclined to assume. The fact is that we have been systematically trained since 1939 to be aware of this sort of thing; and if necessary, disguised in uniforms and wrapped round with improbable implements like parachutes and daggers, to play at it ourselves. In the 15th to 17th centuries we would have been trained to discover witchcraft in much the same systematic manner, in the 19th century business opportunities. Consequently cloaks and daggers surround us as flying saucers surround Americans. But this rehabilitation of the Baden-Powell way of looking at life is not the work of the respectable rebels of the Thirties, but as might be expected, of the conservative side, which always finds it impossible to understand a world that is slipping out of its grasp except in terms of sinister conspiracies by inscrutable orientals, and which, in any case, contains people with a fondness for certain forms of semi-mystical mumbo-jumbo. However, this is not the place to write that study of *Kipling, John Buchan and the British governing class since Queen Victoria's Jubilees* which is badly needed. We, the rebels, had to wait for our real training in the sinister approach to life until we got into the genuine John Buchan fancy-dress world of the British army. Of course we pitied ourselves a little in the Thirties, for we all thought we should be killed in the next war with gasmasks on, a claustrophobic but common fear. We also developed certain local forms of romanticism, but no more than one develops at that age (or later) about any activity which is interesting and appears to be important, like love, or following one's trade.

Saving the world, therefore, did not seem to us to be a separate kind of activity, boring, conspiratorial or otherwise, but a normal part of life. Naturally, some of us specialised in it and spent a good deal of time on it, mainly, but not exclusively, in C.U.S.C. and the numerous other political clubs of the left. Most people simply did a certain amount of world-saving as a matter of course, as one goes to concerts and parties. In fact, we distributed our emotions and energies evenly over the public and private sectors of the landscape. That is why one may still hear survivors of the Thirties talk in the same way about their love-affairs and the Spanish Republic, their personal humiliations and Munich. Since everyone's supply of emotions is, for practical purposes, unlimited, this did not mean stinting either the public or the private sectors; especially not in Oxford. Cambridge showed some Cromwellian tendencies to puritanism and monogamy among the more specialised politicians, though rejecting the sectarian, not to say impracticable, advice of a local bolshevik song-writer—now an American anti-communist—to liquidate love until the Revolution. Politics therefore did not make life narrower. On the contrary, it gave it more variety and interest. We got from it that third dimension of living which the French, the Italians, the Greeks and all other civilized peoples have always recognised to be desirable. (Who, given the choice, would not find life more entertaining in the Paris of Louis Philippe, which was full of politics, than in the Paris of Louis XIV which had practically none?) Our politics did not deprive anybody who wished to live a purely private and internal life of the possibility of doing so. Plenty of people did so. If they felt uncomfortable about it, as some of them did, they could easily square their consciences by giving tins of condensed milk for Basque child refugees or, a favourite way round the problem, by joining a pacifist group. On the other hand we avoided that strain and unhappiness which today frustrates people whose instinct is to feel about world affairs exactly as we did then, but who find it impossible to translate their feelings into action, as we did.

This, of course, is a fantastic way of looking at the matter. We did not take to politics for therapeutical or aesthetic reasons, but because we wanted to fight Fascism, War and the Slump, causes which nobody defended then, even the slump having lately been abandoned by the economists. As this is not a political discussion, I do not propose to defend us against the charges that we were naïve, optimistic, unmindful of the dangers of totalitarianism and so on. I will merely state that a drinking man, offered a glass of whisky for every intelligent university man or woman between the ages of 18 and 30 who could then be got to defend British foreign policy (which chiefly infuriated us), would have been a long way from delirium tremens. This for the obvious reason that the policy was almost impossible to defend intelligently (though the job has been done). A glance at most of those who today claim never to have fallen victims to the 'illusions of the 'Thirties' should confirm this. The great majority of politically-minded British and American intellectuals of that generation may have been wrong, but it was in good company. However, starry-eyed or not, we had two advantages over our successors. First, our beliefs had no great cash value, and we were on the whole not distracted in our activities by the hopes and fears of careerism. In Britain at any rate, the chance of breaking into politics through any of the major parties was negligible until

1945; nor did we take it. The undergraduate socialists of the later 1930's have provided hardly any government ministers. One of the few exceptions, Christopher Mayhew at Oxford, was even then an anomaly, being one of the two supporters of Transport House then known in the student socialist movement. Oxford has since provided a fair batch of back-bench Labour M.P.s. Cambridge not even that. (Cambridge, on the other hand, has supplied communist leaders for India, Ceylon, the Middle East and Britain.) Second, we were not handicapped by being allied to the ape-men. One of the things which made our lives much happier was the fact that people like American Republican senators and S.S. generals were strictly on the other side. It is true that we did not take some of them as seriously as we might have done. But then we did not yet know what James Thurber has lately pointed out, that 1952 should be shaking in its shoes at the thought of the sort of Congressman whom 1937 regarded as a corny joke. Perhaps I may add that nobody on our side then dropped burning petrol jelly on civilians, even Asian ones. In fact, when some Nazi airmen dropped what is by modern standards a grotesquely small quantity of high explosive on a Basque village, the international uproar was such that General Franco's spokesmen denied that they had anything to do with it.

With all these advantages, it may be suggested, we should have been a generation of world-beaters. This does not follow. However, for all I know we may have been, because the 'Thirties produced and formed a good crop of brilliant natural scientists, the trade which nowadays probably attracts the most imaginative talents, provided they can learn some mathematics. In other respects I doubt whether we were anything special. Should we have been? We did not have more talented people among us than earlier Cambridge generations and rather fewer than later ones; for in our day not so many scholarships and awards were given. We were pretty much the same as you, though we listened to Count Basie rather than Humphrey Lyttelton, were not yet stuck on Victorian Gothic, hitch-hiked less—the sport was only invented in the later 'Thirties—had many more Van Gogh reproductions on our walls, still included a lot of people whose social life and tastes were those of the 'Twenties, and had rather less religion about the place than there seems to be today. We had technically worse undergraduate journals with much smaller circulations; indeed some of our *Grantas* were appalling. In return, we had heroes—John Cornford, who was killed at Cordova, leaving behind a dark, handsome photo on many of our mantelpieces; also a symbol of the villainy we were certain one day to overcome, Neville Chamberlain's rolled umbrella. We composed more parodies and political songs than people today, but our Union speeches, film-criticisms and party conversations were quite indistinguishable from present ones, except on very close inspection. In fact, Cambridge today is recognisably the same place as it was then.

It may turn out that, as individuals, we achieved more or less than our predecessors or than the present generation, but there is not much point in such comparisons. All one can say is that, collectively, we achieved some things never before done in Cambridge, and rarely done in western universities after 1848, when their students ceased to be the typical revolutionaries of the European continent, and became, in the main, supporters of the centre and right wings in politics. (In the General Strike of 1926, for instance, most Cambridge and Oxford students either blacklegged or were prepared to blackleg.) Against the immense dead weight of tradition, of authority, and of the more numerous neutrals and conservatives, we transformed the general atmosphere of undergraduate life as previous generations of rebels had not done. This achievement may be admired for its technical difficulty, like the climbing of King's Chapel, even if one does not see much purpose in it. We, however, did see some purpose in it and this gave us an advantage over the present. We knew (and know) some things which only a political generation of the left can learn. We know, for example, that the *Magic Flute* is not merely another opera like *La Bohème* only better. We know what it is about, and what moved Mozart when he wrote it, for Mozart shared our type of enthusiasm for what Shaw once called the 'sentimental dogmas of life, liberty and the pursuit of happiness'. It is entirely possible to manage without this enthusiasm, as it is possible to refrain from making love or having children. One need not even be conscious of missing anything. Indeed, those who do not feel in their bones what we learned in Cambridge fifteen years ago, the desire to build a good society, and the confidence that it can be done, will not understand what all the noise is about. We, the unregenerate survivors of the 'Thirties are not therefore trying to get 1952 to imitate us, as we might (if employed in advertising agencies) sell you desirable goods. What we have is not to be acquired like detergents, Jamaica rum, a wide reading in the works of Proust, or any other aid to gracious living. We merely state that, on further reflection, we still don't feel homesick for any other Cambridge generation, before or after ours, or anybody else's lifetime, except ours. Thank you, we are quite happy as we are.

15 November 1952

In Defence of the 'Fifties

RONALD BRYDEN

If ever a generation shied at barricades, ours is the one. Mr Hobsbawm has implied it, with a faint sniff, and levelly we agree. But though we find constant, Lawrentian emphasis of the fact unnecessarily surgical, by heaven, we have blood in our veins! We tolerate almost everything—even our elders—but when they begin to snipe at three-year-olds, we reach awkwardly but vengefully for our fowling pieces. One more subtle sneer, thinly veiled as comparison, one more ill-concealed gibe thrown in the milk-teeth of our young but promising decade, and we may hire the appropriate wigs and culottes from London costumiers, hang effigies from hastily-erected Emmett lamp-posts and parade through Cambridge in our Edwardian taxis waving torches and singing 'She was Poor but She was Honest' in a menacing manner. Detractors have been warned.

The 'Fifties thus far may be poor, but at least they are honest. With a shallow pretence of rehabilitating his chosen decade, the 'Thirties, Mr Hobsbawm has impugned that honesty, accusing us of aesthetic dilettantism, social amorality and political vacuity. The 'Thirties, he claims—adding, by implication, 'in contrast to the present'—did not flee to bury their face in the lap of the past, hiding from an austere reality among the Offenbach-and-ostrich-feathers of an illusory *belle époque*. They did not, he hints maliciously, fiddle away strength and integrity while the world burned in painting an ivory tower varying shades of *fin-de-siècle* mauve. Yes, he means us.

Describing the 'Thirties, he sketches the portrait of an heroic age, heroic even in bluff denial of its own heroism. It was an age, we gather, of strong minds and strong hearts, when Cambridge undergraduates loved and sang, worked and fought, with the joyous intensity of burning political conviction. Perhaps we are not blandished by his picture of party cells in every college, shelves groaning with Lenin and John Strachey, and the handing out of pamphlets on K.P. But we do not deny the brightness which enfolds the small company of young men who sailed, like Tennyson's Apostles a century earlier, to fight in the rubble of Madrid and under the blue skies of Estremadura. It is a picture which indeed dwarfs us, making us aware of the deeper inadequacy of pipe-stemmed trousers.

But are these the real 'Thirties? Mr Hobsbawm will not be sentimental even about his own past, but is it not possible that the 'Thirties were sentimental about the present? To those of us who observed them from prams and knew no more of their fashions than the buttoned-seat romper, they naturally seemed spacious days; but looking back we begin to wonder if we were not imposed upon. In retrospect, the 'Thirties look like a long series of hunts for Great White Whales, inspired less by Promethean humanism than by infatuation with size for its own sake which savours of megalomania.

What were the monuments of the 'Thirties? One calls to mind the *Queen Mary* and the *Normandie*, the *Hindenburg* and the *Graf Zeppelin*, the Dnieper Dam and Grand Coulee, autostradas and autobahnen, the Maginot Line and the iceberg cubes of apartments towering over the avenues of Berlin and Hamburg. Hilversum and Radio City, the thousand-page best seller, the four-hour film, the Olympics, the World's Fair, the eyes of Joan Crawford and the Biggest Aspidistra in the World—England's last glimpse of the 'Thirties today seems

symbolic : a school of barrage balloons browsing on the grass
of Hyde Park like enormous silver sea-cows, their half-deflated,
puddingy folds sagging in the sun.

Mr Hobsbawm tells us that in the 'Thirties they mixed
love and art and politics in one heady cocktail. To us it looks
as if they had confused all three with mere dimension, and it
sounds not so much intense as Freudian. For us, the 'Thirties
seem to be summed up in Orson Welles' *Citizen Kane*, and
their private life in the image of the gloomy publisher and his
wife sitting by their thirty-foot hearth. Of course, Cambridge
politics were all against the colossi, sworn enemies of Goering
and Big Business with their five miles of tanks in Berlin, five
miles of battleships at Spithead. But in opposition they built
a colossus of their own, the sun-bronzed, eyeless giant in the
blue boiler-cap who clenched a ham-like fist in a thousand
proletarian posters. The style of Dos Passos and *The Grapes of
Wrath* seems a little bloated and *fade* now. It looks to us from
here as if even politics in the 'Thirties were part of the general
quest for Leviathan.

Of course, we were given remedial treatment by the 'Forties,
when the pendulum swung the other way with a bong. They
were the decade of the Little Man, the Little People who
really won the war. On the stage we were exposed to Mr
Coward's *This Happy Breed*, on the air to J. B. Priestley.
Popular songs dealt with the Little Things which Really
Matter, which advertisers exhorted us to bear in mind until
they reappeared in the shops. Publishers found a new market
for Little Dorrit and Little Nell, now approved even by little
magazines, while on the other hand Ronald Searle was inventing his little monsters for *Lilliput*. Politicians praised the small
householder, the tiny folk at home, and the infinitesimal
butter-ration. Perhaps it was because the word large immediately suggested destruction, the huge wrecks of the German
cities or the mushroom shadows over the Pacific—significantly,
the big news of the Bikini explosion was the little pig who

swam to safety, and the name of the hapless atoll was given to a minute new bathing-suit. The United Nations eschewed in their publicity any appeal to a planetary consciousness, and concentrated on cosy posters of small Redskins, Chinese, Hollanders and Maoris, wearing national costume and holding hands.

The point is that we of the 'Fifties have lived through the sort of experience Gulliver went through on his first two voyages, and Alice when she nibbled the mushroom. Its main effect is to develop a strong comic sense. Neither Lilliput nor Brobdingnag were in themselves absurd, except to Gulliver, who had visited both. Not that their absurdity reassured him of his own importance; on the contrary, they made him doubt the importance of everything, until it had passed the test of ridicule. The 'Fifties, by their historical position, have been forced into the procedure for determining truth and value recommended by the Earl of Shaftesbury in the reign of Queen Anne: nothing really true or important, he maintained, can really be made absurd—everything else can. To our surprise, we have found that this kind of test can make the predicament of total relativity not only entertaining, but rewarding. We are obliged to the Earl, who was as wise as he was pleasant, and disliked enthusiasm.

We have found that one of the best tests is unexpected confrontation. We admire New College, Oxford, for placing Epstein's Lazarus under their Reynolds window, and are genuinely sad about the window. We took off our hats to the stage-manager of Roy Campbell's meteoric appearance at a small and devoted University literary society, and are delighted by the news that Dr Edith Sitwell is visiting Hollywood. We should like to keep penguins in the fountain of King's main court—we think the chapel could stand it, but are less sure about academic dignitaries. We should like to persuade Marshal Tito to address the National Playing Fields Association, Benjamin Britten to make an opera about Victoria

and Albert instead of Elizabeth and Essex, and Ernest Hemingway to have tea with Enid Blyton. We should like to place a
small neon sign over the side gate of Buckingham Palace,
reading 'Buckingham Palace'.

Sometimes we find that neither subject suffers from juxta-
position, but that together they form a new experience akin
to Surrealism, which we rather admire. It was this kind of
balance which we liked about the '51 Festival, and which
pleases us about those Georgian rows in Kensington painted
like Neapolitan ice cream. In interior decoration, we find it
agreeable to place a Victorian chair or print among the blond
woods and foam rubber, or to hang pastel-tinted antlers on
the wall near a mobile. We like to see old things in new ways.

It is a kind of aesthetic ambiguity which we find peculiarly
attractive, the kind which permits Mr Betjeman to be at once
amused and delighted by St Pancras, Keble Chapel and the
Albert Memorial: a parodying in which parody and thing
parodied combine and produce their effects simultaneously.
The young man in *Les Faux-Monnayeurs* never got around
to painting a moustache on the Mona Lisa; but we have
adapted his principle generally, and find many Mona Lisas
improved by the adornment.

It is this kind of double appreciation which takes us in
flocks to Victorian melodramas and ballad evenings, to
Western films and exhibitions of French Romantic painting,
which leads us to read Ouida and Daphne du Maurier and
Eric or Little by Little. But ours is not simply the heartless
satire of the 1920s—we find Lytton Strachey as vulnerable to
parody as Florence Nightingale. On the whole, our comic
tests have given us a greater respect for the Victorians than
our predecessors had—it is difficult to reduce Tennyson and
George Eliot to absurdity once you begin to read them. When
we have eliminated by humour General MacArthur and the
Red Dean's jam-jars of germs and the *New Statesman* attitude,
we do arrive at a conclusion about Korea, unheroic perhaps by

the standards of the 'Thirties, but perhaps the simplest and best to take about wars.

We do not forget the young man in Forster's *A Room with a View* who lost his soul through inordinate lust for comedy. In the careful weighing of reality and unreality which makes up the comic, it is possible to lean too much on one scale, and we have lost a few souls to laughter for its own sake. They are the men who thought Lifemanship was something to practise rather than detect—we imagine that in other times they would have been Union speakers and makers of apple-pie beds anyway. Others, more tragic, have become trapped in the parody as the hero of *Berkeley Square* was trapped in the past, and loiter in a Dornford Yates dream, wearing without a hint of humorous intention garments reminiscent of the week-end attire of Toad of Toad Hall. We mourn them, but press on.

For on the whole we find the comic instrument our best guarantee of the honesty we desire above all. It is a shallow judgment which mistakes our attitude to the present for frivolity and to the past for romanticism. Or perhaps the judgment of unconfessed romantics too impatient or too cautious to submit their inmost attitudes to the acid test.

Once before there was a state of mind like ours, in the years following 1660: a reaction like ours from twenty years of uncritical earnestness. Dryden's baroque tragedies with their satirical epilogues suggest that the Restoration too found a tickle to the palate in attitudes at once statuesque and absurd; had she been there, they would probably have cast Joyce Grenfell as Lady Macbeth, to see what happened. Like ours, it was an age kind to science, and not above humour in dress and love. We cannot detect that the court of Charles II was made unhappy by its lack of conviction; it was less intense than the court of George Sand in the 1830s, but it sounds more cheerful, and in its way more practical.

Not that we wish to retreat to the age of periwigs and bed-chamber nepotism. We too would be quite satisfied with the present, but for the enthusiasts who would play tug-o'-war with our souls as the Duchess of Portsmouth and the House of Commons did with Charles II's. We expect that we shall forge a new conviction eventually, and then perhaps we shall admire enthusiasm again. But until then, we are from Missouri, and have to be shown. Mr Hobsbawm, or any survivor of the decade of revolution, is welcome to write a modern *Paradise Lost* against us; but we cannot guarantee him that he will get more than ten pounds.

29 November 1952

Elizabeth Barrett Barrett

THOM GUNN

Paper was stuck all over the window panes,
The air was stale with months-old breathing, the floor
Was thick with a dust through which her feet dragged lanes.
Nightly old fee-foh-fum hurtling in the door
Was welcomed, strong tonic, by this invalid,
Who wanted regular things to be all her need.

Yet he came there too, the energetic man,
The young poet Robert Browning, who would breathe
This used-up and dog-nosed air far rather than
The unpondered winds that swept the streets beneath,
To find a pale girl of thirty-nine years old,
Reserved, by comparison with him, and cold.

Between loneliness, he said, and sufficiency
There is a land for crossing, I do not know
Whether we can cross to that perfect liberty.
I myself am shy and would dread to go
Into your presence without a coat, he said,
And ashamed at the thought of your seeing me naked.

But could we not enter a full relationship
Committed together? It need not be motionless.
My spirit according to yours would soar or dip,
I would be naked before your nakedness—?

But she only said with a proper reticence,
Mr Browning, you have my fullest confidence.

Going he carefully left his words behind
Bold and airy chargers stalled in his stead
Less for her use than to keep him in her mind,
Masculine, brighteyed, whiskered. I will, she said,
Completely resign, so change, and when I change
Risk finding my only value was being strange.

So she exiled all but him, Browning, from her care:
Her very father's safe power dwindled now.
She lifted her lover's questions from the air
And pressed them to her white skin, wondering how
Firmness belonged to the leaping shapes of breath
That nosed, indeed, a creature marked for death.

Yet after the flight could the question not lie dozing
In her pastures, never bothering to spring,
On the lack a look of breezy movement imposing
With his tail, but needing the horsefly's unkind sting
To goad him on through this country of content
To do all he had meant and she had meant!

And there would be no insistence in his embrace,
No certainty where his mind was, for below
A kindly deception filling out the face
He might be easy that he need not show
Continual proof. That could be worse to endure
Than these blind window panes, where she was sure.

1953

Faber and Faber: A Fifth Quartet

JULIAN JEBB

I

It is my duty,
A strange and honourable duty,
Reaping dust from the dead wind,
To put you gentlemen in mind
Of the Affairs of Faber and Faber.
Thus we are congregate here in the solemn
Perusal of the Company's Business,
In Russell Square, where, in discoloured
Basements the domestic plies his labour,
And we
With easy smiles and clasping hands,
Consider our gains and our losses.

II

In the middle of the way
Between Spring and Autumn,
Between dying
And death;
I have calculated and observed
The seasonal fluctuation.
The withered roses strewn in the gutter,
The soft note of the February blackbird,
Have commented upon our financial progress.
There has been oppression and fulfilment,

E

Concern and achievement;
The intolerable burden of the excess-profits tax,
The obsequious apathy of the booksellers:
The librarians, armed with rubber-stamps,
Empurple all the novels on their shelves.

III

The undergraduate with a scarf
Gives a long and hearty laugh,
But in his heart there twists a knife
That would deprive him of his life.

In his gaslit basement reading
Sits the student with his Pound;
Thoughts from thoughts in constant breeding,
His feet placed firmly on the ground.

The themes presented in a lecture
Are subject to urbane conjecture;
The constable is on his beat,
The fog is crooked in the street.

IV

But that was, to some extent, a diversion,
A way round to the point of beginning.
April was the cruellest month
Few copies of my work sold.
But March will be clean this year,
Welcoming the publication of my Play
The Confidential Clerk,
An undistinguished voyage into the
Much visited territory
Of mistaken identity.
(Shall I follow the deception of the crush bar
Into the first world of critical abuse?)

Herbert Read has regaled us,
In a profusion of commendable obscurity,
With descriptions of modern man,
Of brass and bronze.
Hardly an economic proposition.
I know quite a lot about poets
And I think that Roy Campbell is a strong,
                                        brown poet,
Sullen untamed and intractable.
Sand, heat and blood
Marketable qualities,
And for the most part, publishable.

Thus we have travelled the accustomed ground;
We have arrived at the point where we once were.
Where?
The beginning? The end?
Most likely of all,
The middle.

24 April 1954

One Man's Week

NICHOLAS TOMALIN

MONDAY

Last night the newspapers struck. Everyone has been very smug with the realisation of just how unpleasant and uncovered their tube train neighbours looked. Also there is a disinclination to work. No one knows whether tonight's paper will in fact be printed.

At lunchtime we go down to the King and Keys. William Hickey and the Diplomatic Correspondent between them make me drink seven half pints of best bitter, which is too much for mid-day. We talk with embarrassing sincerity of the malaise of human kind. Then they pack me off to find a story. For an hour I wander hazily down Fleet Street trying to conjure up something in either the living-history or the history-in-stone line. Nothing comes that hasn't very obviously come before. Then, at about three o'clock, I discover where the Trafalgar Square pigeons live.

This is not where you might think. Those are starlings. The pigeons live beyond the Canadian Pacific buildings, in Carlton House Terrace. There is a bombed out palatial residence there —Nos. 18–23—where they cluster, sleep, and drop droppings on to the rotten parquet beneath them. One entire wall is still pilastered, obviously the remnants of a ritzy ballroom. Pigeons fight for perches on the guilded acanthus leaves. There is a constant coming and going as they fly across to the square for food, water, or company.

This, I say to myself, is without doubt today's William Hickey column. It has everything. Human interest, do-you-know-your-London interest, snob-historical-interest (Gladstone, Eden, and Ribbentrop lived about there), where-else-but-in-England interest, not to mention simple pigeon-interest. Combined with the twenty-five pigeons I saw perching on Reg Butler's *Birdcage* three weeks ago and the seven swans I saw marching up and down the mudflats last year it makes the perfect image.

Having collected background material and local colour—apparently Mr Creech Jones, or some later Home-Secretary, has cleaned up the Trafalgar Square except for two licensed pigeon-feed sellers who store forty sacks of dried peas in the gentlemen's lavatory of the tube station, earn ten pounds a day, have factories in Ealing packaging the peas, and are worried acutely by their income tax—I tell myself to walk, not run, to the nearest taxi rank.

Back at work I steal Drusilla Beyfus's typewriter and feel one of the famous. She is furious, but can't recognise it when she comes to look. My boss is disconsolately pecking out a story on King's Road, Chelsea—the most fascinating thoroughfare in the world.

'What have you got?' he asks me.

'Where the pigeons live,' I say, just too casually.

'Oh . . . good,' he says, and doesn't even ask me what I mean. So I stop writing, and wander off to help the sub-editor who is frantically attempting to carry our readers over the yawning gap in the comic strip narrative caused by the strike. I write two for him. The first reads: 'Jeff's *Sabre*, carrying through its steep arc, has caught a Martian disk with its wingtip. The interplanetary craft, mortally stricken, plunges towards the Australian desert. Now read on. . . .' The second: 'My, what a to-do! Here's the nasty man changed the name on Nigel's magic yacht, and Pepito's nose refuses to go dry. . . . Still, here comes the parrot man to their help—.'

The *Mirror*, so I hear, will publish their strip cartoons in duplicate. . . .

TUESDAY

We were published but William Hickey is still unsettled. He sits moodily in the back of taxis, fingering his umbrella and talks of civilisation gone sick. We go everywhere by taxi, but if we go to the Savoy it is an expense account convention that we call it the Dorchester.

In the evening it is a party at the Dorchester. There we meet Kingsley Martin and Mistinguette. Mistinguette is in England for the publication of her book on the sexiness of her past life. Until she heard that the newspaper strike was irrevocably over she refused to say a word to anyone. Sitting immobile on a low divan she looks like something exhumed. She is eighty. Terrified, we both leave.

Next the party is at the Watergate. We meet Ada Reeve, who says it is not true that Gaiety Girls drank champagne out of their slippers, or at least that *she* could only have done such a thing had she been really very much the worse for wear. . . . Leaving this tit-bit for the *Evening Standard* Night Reporting Corps we use Ada Reeve as an excuse for a dithyramb on Brixton: 'Dear old Brixton. . . . I remember trams rattling along the causeway . . . . the sweet shop where mother used to buy those liquorish lollipops . . . . the old Gaiety, with the best show in town, etc., etc.' The dots—always four—are essential to the William Hickey style, mark it as the only daily column which pauses to think as it goes along.

About Mistinguette we are brutally frank.

WEDNESDAY

Opportunity knocks peremptorily and unsettlingly. The editor summons me through a little secretary quite as terrified as I. As I come into the office—which I haven't seen since I was originally told that if I was good to the *Daily Express* it would be good to me—he fires a question at me. The editor is about the only man in the world who can fire a question with conviction. With him it is efficiency, not affectation. The question is whether I am a Dickie Valentine fan.

I fire back no. In fact I have never heard the name before.

'Well, we have to work the new appeal to youth. You're a youth, could you explain what he could mean to you if you were a fan?'

Both greatness and ambition require a lie here. 'Yes I could. Tricky job, but possible.'

'Do it.'

Dickie Valentine turns out, from his old cuttings, to be a crooner, as I had suspected. His appeal to youth seems to be quite simple and straightforward sex. From his pictures he looks like Billy Graham, a sexual Billy Graham.

During the afternoon I try to think up phrases to explain this creditably. Phrases about tribal rites, up from the common people, romantic abstractions, and neat analogies with Espresso coffee. None of these ring as true as they might.

In the evening to the Chiswick Empire. In the dressing room a pleasant undistinguished young man with blue bathing trunks underneath his midnight blue evening dress. Outside a screaming mob.

On stage he carries a little stick microphone and walks nonchalantly to and fro, occasionally fitting it into slots so that he can wave his arms. Every time he comes to one side a girl in an ornate box screams, throws herself forward, is pulled back by her companions—also screaming—and then buries herself beneath a pile of their bodies. By the time they have sorted themselves out he is back again.

In front of me two girls sit, with their hands intertwined. One uses nail varnish the other not. All four hands as they clutch are white with tension. As they can't clap they jump up and down, banging the floor with their legs. I notice the pit drummer always helps the banging and clapping by hitting his tom-toms with his hands during moments of applause.

Dickie Valentine imitates a series of people of whom I learnt this afternoon. Billy Eckstein, Billy Daniels, Mario Lanza, and—known before—Johnny Ray. During 'Cry' he throws a handkerchief to the box girls. They fight for the next quarter of an hour. His voice is obviously out of tune at times.

All in all the most amazing thing about the show is the preponderance of lavatory jokes, and the way the audience constantly repeat each one amongst themselves until they understand it, then laugh loudly.

Afterwards we all go round to the stage door. Dickie promises us seventy-five signed portraits; so we wait while he signs them, panting in anticipation, squealing, squealing all the way.

Then the crowd begin to grumble. A very small man comes out, completely bald, carrying a 'cello. The crowd laughs at him. One wag in Edwardian clothes says, 'Here he is!', and the back of the queue push us forward round the little man. The squeals are unbearable. 'Dickie, Dickie!' shouts the rear. The wag starts to embrace the little man, to roars of laughter. The little man drops his 'cello. Another wag carries it down the queue shouting, 'Here he is, here he is!', with the little man trying to loose himself. A policeman gets the 'cello back, and the little man scuttles off, but then, forgetting something, has come back to the stage door to repeat the whole process again. The second time I leave with him.

I shall use the article I tried to write without seeing Mr Valentine.

THURSDAY

Because some girl is murdered, the *Express* has a Pyramid Club story on its front page. Ten days ago I wrote a story on pyramid clubs. Hickey thought it was publicity and turned it down. I had big names, intrigue, sparkle, all an employer could want—now they spend a full front-page column in explaining the game. . . .

What is the biggest rub is the quote from Mark Boxer, my own sponsor. They might have asked me.

I ring up Mark to discover that he did not say what they say he said. In particular the enthusiastic statement about pyramid clubs bringing one into contact at parties with all sorts of exciting new people such as débutantes, coloured gentlemen, and barrow boys. He has already been rung up three times by strange voices who hear that he arranges nice parties with eight coloured gentlemen, and would he please arrange one for them. . . .

At lunch, to add a royal element to the seamy day, someone offers me a photograph of Princess Margaret in bed for £350. I refuse.

FRIDAY

Up to four thirty no one had any ideas. Then we decided to go and see Feliks Topolski in his new studio under Hungerford bridge. He has used large windows—lent him by 'David' —from the Coronation Abbey Annex. Otherwise the décor is vulgar. All bear rugs, weathered cherubs, Sheraton tables and hanging sheets. Vulgar, I think, but Mr Hickey is tremendously taken, and we stand about drinking good sherry out of tumblers, talking at cross purposes and, each for totally different reasons, having to resist an inclination to giggle.

Our column is headed: 'Underneath the Arches with a Genius. . . .'

SATURDAY

On the one free day of the week we sit in an Espresso bar and I am laughing campily over a menu footnote: 'Capucino, named after those peculiar brown habits of the Capucini order of monks' when someone I haven't seen for ten years approaches us. He wears a wing collar. 'What are you doing?' I ask him. 'I sell' . . . pause . . . 'space,' he murmurs, and moves mysteriously away.

We meet five other friends during the evening. London is the smallest and most tightly interwoven of all small worlds.

When I ride in a taxi I can lean out of the window and shout at friends in upper windows, then be gone by the time they look out.

Similarly with monotonous regularity I meet someone in the Holland Park tube lift. Usually a man called Beamish with whom I once had what he calls a mad party drinking Pomagne in the Festival Gardens.

Girls at work know men who had affairs with girls at school. Old dormitory enemies work for the *Daily Mail*. C's landlord, who is married to the sister of a Cambridge friend, once taught art there. My ex-fiancée can watch him have his breakfast across two back gardens every morning. Her pet famous man is my landlord, whose father in his turn knew C's mother in Welwyn Garden City, and whose wife's aunt is the mother of the girl with whom the man who was next to me on the B.B.C. General Trainee lists is in love with. Next door is a girl I interviewed at a banquet the week before last. I have calculated that the odds against such an involved coincidence, assuming the population of Greater London to be 12,000,000 and that fate has not deliberately brought us together, is about seven hundred million to one. But as I said it's a small world. Rather embarrassingly so.

Similarly it is unnerving to work in very mundane circumstances cheek by jowl with people who otherwise one might think famous. Osbert Lancaster, Artie, Eve Perrick, Morley Richards, Sefton Delmer, Basil Cardew, Leonard Mosley, Anne Edwards, Rene McColl, oh yes, and Nicholas Phipps, all household names to the mass readership of this world, and yet all sat in one vast neon-lighted room quarrelling gently over typewriters and tea, and making jokes about the sex lives of the typists. If this is how the other half lives I am glad I don't.

SUNDAY

Today we go to the Savoy to see Chaplin. He had arranged a quiet interview with Cassandra and Hickey, but the Savoy

Press Office had wind of the arrangement and secretly sent out invitations to every paper in London in order to get wider publicity. Cassandra sulks throughout the press conference, as it has now become.

Chaplin seems frightened. He is old, and very white haired. He sits everyone down and is nervously affable, shaking hands and making jokes.

He has come to give away £2,000 to charity. No one knows which one; so one journalist keeps on petulantly and crudely trying to find out. He plugs away at trick questions, interrupting the other speaker who is talking about ponies and children, questions like: 'You *did* say you were giving the money to Dr Barnardo's didn't you sir?' Chaplin isn't annoyed, but we are.

At moments his face lights up with some kind of gaiety. He looks more like the *Modern Times* Chaplin, which I saw a few days before, than the *Limelight* Chaplin. Seven men protect him, mostly French, or Germans who speak in guttural English making arrangements with photographers.

He is not to give any money to America. All the reporters scribble furiously. His next film he says will be a light hearted satire on American life. Reporters scribble. Very obviously, for the first time, scarcely any of the Press like Mr Chaplin any more. I can't quite see what difference a Stalin Peace Prize should make.

Mr Chaplin also says he wants to wander the streets of Brixton where he used to live. We can't do Brixton again; so we tactfully slang Mr Chaplin. This is, anyway, the *Express* line.

The *Express* line never obtrudes itself more firmly or dictatorially than this. Circumstances and general attitudes seem to dictate the distortions of the modern world. I suppose I'm being corrupted, I can't quite tell.

6 November 1954

Tea with Wallace Kennedy

GEOFFREY STRICKLAND

During my first year in the university
I was privileged by a visit
From Wallace Kennedy
The distinguished poet, novelist and critic.

His tones were rich and Caribbean,
Through the portentous gloom
His conversation edited
In close neat type the afternoon.

Intense and confidential, cosmic,
It took in Kafka, James and Gide,
Accepted toast and tea, then gave his views
On the *Kenyon* and *Connecticut Reviews*.

'A liberal public needs its guesses
By definition; old Valéry
Had a shrewd grey eye',
He offered before leaving,

His intonations evoking
Distant breakers on the shores of time
And the march of printing presses.

Gadfly, 1954

A Dialogue

BAMBER GASCOIGNE

An American travelling-salesman is sitting at a bar; he is already drowsy-drunk, so that his words and gestures are blurred.

    Enter a prim little boy, in shorts and white shirt.

The Boy: Excuse me, sir.

The American: Yeah?

The Boy: There are two gentlemen waiting for you, sir.

The American: Let 'em wait. I ain't finished drinking.

(Pause)

    But what sort of guys are these?

The Boy: Quite old gentlemen, sir.

The American: And you say there are two of them?

The Boy: Yes, sir.

The American: Yeah, that's them. They been waiting some time, I guess: but they'll keep. I'm gonna sell 'em a life insurance policy. They sure need it.

(Pause)

    Do you need a life insurance policy?

The Boy: No thank you, sir.

The American: Have a gin fizz then?

The Boy: No thank you, sir.

The American: Don't drink?

The Boy: No, sir.

The American: Say.

(*Pause*)

Do these guys look kinda ragged?

The Boy: Yes, sir.

The American: Yeah, that's them all right.

(*Pause*)

The Boy: Shall I take them a message, sir?

The American: Yeah, sure. Say I'll be along.

The Boy: When, sir?

The American: Shucks, kid, I dunno. It don't matter. They'll wait. But say tomorrow night. Tell 'em I'll be along tomorrow night.

The Boy: What name shall I give, sir?

The American: Eh? Oh yes. Godot. Plain Mr Godot.

26 November 1955

One Man's Week

ANON.

MONDAY

Arrival. We drove up to the locked doors, rang, and were admitted into the pleasantly painted hall. Here we sat and waited until the staff were ready to examine me. I said good-bye to my friend and followed the nurse into the examination ward, where I undressed, hearing the noisy sound of gear-changing as the car went back down the drive. There followed a physical examination and some questions of which I have a somewhat scattered memory. 'Are your teeth your own?' I was asked. I thought for a moment of saying that I was buying them on the Hire Purchase, but decided against it. 'I haven't got them all,' I replied a little stiffly, 'but such as I have are certainly my own.' 'Do you believe in telepathy?' was another question. It took me by surprise. 'Well, I hardly know—I'm quite prepared to believe in telepathy. I haven't thought about it very much. I believe the evidence is quite good—' 'Thank you. Can you explain for me the meaning of the proverb: "A bird in the hand is worth two in the bush"?' I explained it, clumsily but adequately. 'And "All that glisters is not gold"?' I explained that too. 'I see, that will do. Take him to bed, nurse.'

I spent the rest of the day in bed.

TUESDAY

I moved into the ward where live others on the same treatment and began to learn the routine. The day begins at 6.30, when we are woken and injected. We rise and wash, come back and make our beds, and get back into bed. The injection has the effect of sending one into a deep unconscious state. I am not yet on full treatment and so do not go into this, but lie listening to the others snoring and grunting. They are roused from unconsciousness by having glucose poured down through funnels in the nostrils. Some however do not revive very quickly. Fred for instance takes a long time to come round. A nurse busily pours down the glucose. 'Good morning, Fred,' shouts another. Fred doesn't answer. They slap his feet, pour in some more glucose and try again. 'Good morning, Fred. What's my name, Fred?' By this time the floor round Fred's bed is crowded with nurses, doctors in white coats and rimless spectacles, and trolleys of equipment. The glucose is being pumped in now through a syringe about the size of a bicycle pump, which wheezes like an old pair of bellows. Fred is screened off, but the chorus round his bed rises. 'Good morning, Fred—Where's that syringe nurse—Wake up Fred boy, it's morning—Breakfast time, Fred—Take away that funnel— Come on Fred, you know me, it's Chris—Good morning, Fred.' Their efforts are rewarded, at the height of the chorus there comes a gasp from Fred. 'G'morning.'

We have breakfast in bed, followed by a bath. One rarely wants breakfast, but it is part of the treatment. Then we dress, sweep and dust the room, and join the other patients in the day-room. It is almost time for lunch. We have meals and spend the evenings with the other patients, but otherwise we lead slightly separate lives. We spend all the time together as a group, whatever the afternoon activities, and there must always be a nurse with us. But the greatest bond of all is glucose. Glucose revives us in the morning, glucose is on our cereal at breakfast, we wash spattered drops of glucose from the walls when we clean our ward. We are called away specially after lunch to have glucose tea, we suck glucose sweets all afternoon and wherever we go we take a tumbler, and a bottle of glucose.

In the afternoon I had further medical examinations, and so got out of the group for a little. After tea I tried to read a novel I had brought with me, and then became involved in a game of snooker. I was not sorry to go to bed at the appointed time of half past eight.

WEDNESDAY

In the afternoon there was a football match against another hospital. We are very near the top of the league, which is not surprising as the other teams come from ordinary physical hospitals, whereas our players are not only fit but can be counted on to show a certain low cunning in front of goal. Anyway, we thrashed these representatives of the maim, the halt and the blind by 11–2, and I had a very easy game at right back.

THURSDAY

Our group went for a walk in the afternoon. The pace of the group is the pace of the slowest, and it was a very slow procession that made its way through the flat, wintry country-side down to the village. Here it became even slower as we drifted from shop to shop, buying sweets and icecreams, for we are encouraged to eat. On the way back we made a half-hearted attempt to overtake a party of old-age pensioners in high-heeled shoes, but it came to nothing. But we livened up enough to arrive at the canteen before it closed.

In the evening a party was held in the main building. It was quite a brisk affair and made me admire the staff more than ever. Afterwards I settled down to a game of whist. The first hand was spoiled when it was found that each player had a king of hearts, but we sorted out the pack and started again. I am no whist player, but the standard was not high : the man on my right not only trumped his partner's winning trick, but trumped it with the ace. This incident depressed me out of all proportion to its importance, I can't say why.

In the afternoon we saw a film in the main building. They were showing *Rob Roy*: there were a few interruptions, and between reels someone stood up in the audience and harangued us. I could not hear him distinctly enough to tell whether he was a Scotsman particularly stirred by the action, or whether he had some other reason.

In the evening some Quakers from the district gave a concert—very musicianly, very civilised, very enjoyable. They were warmly applauded.

There is no treatment over the weekend and most people go away. There was an air of suppressed excitement from early morning: the queue to wash was more impatient than ever and cleaning the ward was done with much more haste and vigour. One old man was so impatient that he got up at half-past five to look for his boots: the poor fellow had still not been fetched by nine o'clock. My own arrangements went blessedly smoothly: I was signed for and taken away just after nine.

I found a distinct atmosphere of depression on return. Everyone looked forward immensely to the weekend as a relief from the week, but it is often an anti-climax for the disease of course doesn't stop, and may even be excited by the break in routine. One of my friends had had to come back in the middle, and had gone to bed. Another had not been able to get away, and was very depressed by a letter from his girl friend and the prospect of not being able to get home the next week. In our ward at bedtime no one felt like sleep, in spite of the sleeping pills. The conversation soon became lively, and ranged wide and deep. We discussed how far the doctors really knew what they were doing, why it was that food always tasted much better at weekends, the ethics of suicide, whether it was feasible to pinch a crane that was working down the road and which someone wanted to keep in his locker. Sooner or later we always came back to life in the hospital. Fred summed up the discussion. 'Here, you know what I think?' he asked at last, raising himself on one elbow. 'No, Fred, what do you think?' 'I think there are a lot of queer things going on round here.'

18 February 1956

'Noel Annan was very kind'

MARK BOXER

I first saw Anthony de Hoghton eating by himself in the reigning Cambridge restaurant. I retain a distinct picture of him tackling an elaborate savoury. He was round, pink, and blond, verging in fact on the albino. He would wobble when he was angry with a waiter, but not flabbily; it was a stiff wobble, like a jelly in its first moments out of the jelly mould.

He had a younger brother in Trinity and I probably met him there. He spoke forcefully and yet pedantically with a curious roundness of speech as if he had a liqueur chocolate in the back of his mouth (he probably had).

I was impressed by his erudition and his style; he did not suffer from the English habit of concealing his intelligence. He was very good company. His knowledge was recondite, ornate, and particularly strong in French literature. Altogether he was a new and fascinating figure for me: black sheep, lapsed Catholic, with a conversational style that was streaked with sudden bouts of verbal savagery.

We spent a considerable amount of time together during the spring term. He had left Oxford some years before but obviously liked university life. I was coming to the end of my third year. Until now, Simon Raven had filled the role of 'black' friend. Although Simon was still at Cambridge (actively not working for his fellowship), he was losing something of his style. As he himself has recounted, he moved surrep-titiously from guest room to guest room in King's, intermittently borrowing his friends' clothes when his own became too offensive for him. One of the risks that term was to be generously invited to dinner by Simon only to find him wearing your favourite suit. I remember he had mostly given up socks.

Anyway, at the end of term I asked Anthony de Hoghton to guest-edit the first issue of *Granta* for the following term. He accepted.

I arrived for my last summer term to find that Anthony de Hoghton had failed to appear with his promised collection of articles. Eventually a telegram arrived from Paris with a courteous apology for letting us down, but he promised two pieces of his own. These duly arrived.

The first manuscript was a short story of an allegorical nature called 'Freewheeling with Christ'. I have forgotten its exact nature but I quickly decided it was unpublishable. The poem on the other hand I liked. It had considerable dash and spirit. It was on the same theme as an earlier work of his that started: 'God is cranking up his Bentley in the garage.' I thought it was genuine in its feeling and I decided to publish it. It had the authentic de Hoghton sound.

I have heard many explanations for my decision to publish the poem, the most insulting being the canard that there was a 'hole' in the issue and that I put in a poem that I hadn't read. This was far from the case, although I didn't deliberate or worry over the decision. I did however show it to a Catholic assistant editor (all one's friends were assistant editors); and although he didn't care for it he was not unduly perturbed by its inclusion.

It doesn't seem worth printing the whole poem, but there were certain lines that I found striking at the time. The scene is set by the first and second verses:

Let God get up. He snores in bed
With a dirty old stocking wrapped round his head.
The household's all at sixes and sevens,
The dust is thick on his seven heavens.

Let God get up. He's wide awake
Sucking his thumb and calling for cake
His eyes are red and gummed with gold,
If he don't look alive he'll be bought and sold.

The fourth and sixth verse launch the attack:

Let God get up, the slug-a-bed,
Cosmic snail with tortoise head,
Ten arms, five legs and a gross of eyes,
With a do-nothing God I can't sympathize.

You're a silly old thing, I'm telling you straight
You're smelly and ugly and out of date. . .

A few other lines keep up to the same level. For example:

. . . Well the game's up, see, we know your tricks,
You're our favourite at the flicks . . .

But alas, the writer couldn't resist one obvious rhyme to the word 'God', and this probably caused the trouble:

You drunken gluttonous seedy God,
You son of a bitch, you snotty old sod.

I should perhaps at this point make it clear that I have no religious feelings at all. At school I had been asked by the school chaplain not to attend his divinity class as I asked him disturbing questions; but there was no heat in my teasing him and I believe he secretly rather enjoyed it. Although I have always thought there is a very joky side to most religions I have no animus against the Christian religion.

The issue with the poem duly appeared. I was rather proud of the notes on contributors and my caricature of de Hoghton with the caption 'This issue is dedicated to A. de Hoghton without whose help the issue went to press'. The poem caused little fuss as far as we could see; we were all about to take exams and the succeeding issue, an inoffensive travel number, went to press.

Around this time I was interviewed by *Varsity* and the following Saturday they published the information that the final May week *Granta* was to be an 'anti-Coronation' number. I had in fact meant the word to read 'ante' at this stage, although a certain ambiguity was intended. It was the summer of 1953, the year of the Coronation; the press were full of chat about a second Elizabethan age. Eaden Lilley's had put ermine capes round their corset models in their shop windows. . . .

The Cambridge group to which I was attached viewed the royal 'thing' with something near the same scepticism (but I like to feel with rather more style) that Muggeridge and Osborne were to show later. We were certainly planning a rather special number, but eleven years later I can only remember two ideas. A cartoon Coronation Procession was to run through the whole issue, and there was to be a mock cut-out design along cornflake-packet lines captioned 'Make your own Guardsman'. (It is difficult in these heterosexual times to remember how queer everyone seemed to be when the Queen was at her zenith.)

Rumour has it that intelligence of our plans reached the notice of the Vice Chancellor. It was said by various young dons—I now think unfairly—that he hoped as it was Coronation year to do rather better than usual in the New Year's honours list.

The first news of trouble however came from an assistant art editor. He arrived at my rooms in King's with a mad story about policemen and proctors stopping the press at Foister and Jagg to check on the up-coming issue. On investigation the mad story turned out to be true.

My memories of the next few days are difficult to untangle. I remember being ill and my tutor at King's treating the whole thing lightly until he had seen the University authorities, and then realizing it was serious. I was summoned after a few days of doubt to some dim rooms in one of the dimmer colleges, Emmanuel or more probably Christ's. I was rather surprised on entering the Proctors' rooms to find also in attendance a plain-clothes policeman wearing his raincoat indoors. I still consider the Proctors behaved badly by interrogating me in front of the police. By University statute I was bound to answer their questions truthfully. And yet at the same time I inevitably must incriminate myself with the police.

I was accused of blasphemy. This is still a common law offence, though few cases have been brought in this century. However, Noël Annan was very kind; he consulted a barrister on my behalf. He considered, in the unlikely event of a case coming to court, that judgement would probably go against me.

The interview was icy; the punishment was steep. First *Granta* was to be banned for the rest of the year. Secondly I was to be rusticated. I was allowed to finish my exams, but I was to leave Cambridge for the rest of the term.

The Proctors were well within their rights to discipline me. The statutes say (among other injunctions against giving tradesmen promissory notes, discharging fire-arms and taking part in gaming transactions) that they can prevent students 'from practices that are inconsistent with gentlemanly behaviour . . . They take cognizance in general of any viola-

tion of morality and decorum'. They made however two
tactical mistakes. I was instructed not to discuss the affair
with any outside body. 'Outside body' in this instance was
clearly a euphemism for 'the Press'. The injunction I adhered
to. They were not aware however that when the news
inevitably circulated, several undergraduates would be only
too happy to inform the London papers. This would probably
earn a fiver. This was done not only for the money: Cambridge was beginning to be aware of the rat race to come.
Links were being made with possible future employers. I had
myself been approached during the vacation by a star
columnist. I had been entertained in a Sloane Square bar and
offered two pounds for any story of mine that gate-crashed
his column. I only tried once with a story I thought funny
and he didn't. However on this occasion I behaved well; someone else must have rung the papers and suddenly Fleet Street
descended.

Here the Proctors made their second mistake. Presumably
rattled by the sympathy my case was getting, one of them
gave a 'quote' to the press. The senior of the two told *The
Times* and several other papers that the poem was 'uncompli-
mentary to God'. For those with a nose for theology this was
thought about as blasphemous a suggestion as the poem itself.

Inevitably, the affair blew up into a kind of bogus event.
There were protests, a debate in the Union condemning the
Proctors (won 104 to 46). *Varsity* came out with a black
border; a petition was organized. It was signed among other
distinguished figures by E. M. Forster who in his short note
described the Proctors' decision as 'curious'. My college was
very much on my side. The Provost, Sir John Sheppard, wrote
to *The Times* to correct an item and to dissociate King's
from the University authorities' action. Some dons considered
reading the poem into the senate record. According to one
Sunday paper 'A senior don told me: "We feel that this
matter should not have been dealt with by the suppression of

the magazine, although many of us feel the editor should have been disciplined. . . . Feeling is so strong among many of the dons that a plan was on foot today to prevent the two Proctors being re-elected. . . ." This move failed because the necessary 24 hours' notice in writing to the Vice Chancellor before today's meeting was not given.'

I surprised many of my friends by being unexpectedly upset by the affair. Of all the incidents that followed I remember best my fury at a rival editor who shouted his congratulations across Petty Cury ('Surely you have always wanted noto-riety?'). I received many sweet letters and a postbag from free-thinkers living in service flats in Buckingham Gate and elsewhere. I also received a brief note from Anthony de Hoghton asking for the unpublished short story back.

I was not in fact upset about my exams. But I was con-cerned about the finances of the magazine. *Granta* is owned by its editor, and the banning of the magazine with advertis-ing already booked was a considerable financial blow. Some genius however discovered that *Granta* had been started in the late 1880s solely because a magazine called *Gadfly* had been outlawed by the Proctors. It was a simple move to transfer all the advertising and editorial staff. The forth-coming publication of *Gadfly* was announced. I handed the whole affair over to my successor, Nicholas Tomalin, who sharply got together a distinguished list of ex-editors and friends, Glyn Daniel, Charles Fletcher-Cooke, Noël Annan, Ronald Searle, Charles Wintour among them, who agreed to their names appearing on the masthead as nominal editors. 'The assistant editor's decision has been final' read a footnote to an excellent issue which the Proctors did not touch.

The culmination was a 'funeral' organized by some friends. I was rather opposed to the idea, largely because I was afraid it might flop. However an enormous crowd turned up, one newspaper saying three thousand in all, though I suspect it was less than half this number. Hugh Thomas made a striking speech outside King's. I watched from an upper room. It was a splendid affair with a marvellous horse-drawn coffin. One don told me afterwards that during the last funeral he witnessed two undergraduates, sent down for the usual vice, had climbed into the coffin together.

More newspapermen descended and I learnt some of my early lessons about the Press. For the first time I spoke to a reporter. I distinctly remember being caught on my way to lunch by one provincial news-hawk. He said something like 'I suppose you are pretty browned off with the whole caboodle?' At which I must have said 'Yes'. Next day I read 'Mark Boxer said in an exclusive interview yesterday "I am pretty browned off with the whole caboodle".'

I had been told I could not return to Cambridge until June 11th. The proctorial body had apparently chosen this date after consulting its May Week diary and judiciously noticed the date of the last May Ball. This was in fact the King's Ball which was to take place on June 10th. However, the Proctors forgot that Balls are inclined to last rather longer than midnight and I arrived back at my college for its Ball at 12 o'clock.

In the meantime, though I had a job already waiting for me, I joined the *Sunday Express* for three days. There was some idea I should do a series of articles on Oxford and the Sorbonne. I was to be billed as 'the man Cambridge couldn't hold'. I was against this; I wanted to make my early mistakes a little more privately. I suggested instead doing one short piece on distinguished figures who were *leaving* London for the Coronation. This was considered an *Express*-worthy idea. I stuck a pencil in my mouth à la Gully Jimson and rang up several people I knew like E. M. Forster, who as a C.H. I thought would be invited to the Abbey. I then rang up several peers; Bertrand Russell in particular was happy to give a very publishable anti-Coronation quote. A radical bishop also responded well, but he was on the Beaverbrook black list and the reference to him disappeared early on. The story shrank towards the end of the week as they are inclined to on Sunday papers and ended up in Ephraim Hardcastle's column. Dimly I remember feeling that I had covered an aspect of our anti-Coronation issue after all.

2 November 1964

Sentimental Story

MICHAEL FRAYN

The first flying bombs of the war fell on London during the night of 13/14th June, 1944. The following night the gunners shot the wing off a flying bomb on a track well to the south of London. It swerved down into a hillside a hundred yards from our house, and killed a family of five. Our house lost the roof, ceilings and windows.

This is how the happiest month of my life started.

It didn't start immediately. First of all there was the powdered plaster to be beaten out of the carpet, the broken glass to be shaken out of the beds, the roof to be covered with tarpaulins and the front door to be put back on its hinges. Then it rained. The rain soaked the black-out curtains we hung in the empty window-frames, and from them dripped on to the furniture and the floor, picking up unseen plaster dust and making greyish pools everywhere. And while I mopped and wrung out cloths, I had time to think of the five people up the hill who had suffocated to death in their shelter.

But then the weather changed, and men came to nail linen over the windows, so that the house was filled with a white half-light like the pale aura which is reflected on to the ceilings and walls by the snow in winter.

There was nothing left in the house for me to clear up, and the flying bombs no longer frightened me, though I was still excited by them. When the warning sounded, I would take a steel helmet and run up the hill to see if I could see them come over. I would stand by the four piles of rubble which marked the site of the houses destroyed on that first night and put the helmet on to emphasise my sense of danger. Often the bombs would go directly overhead, flying very low, looking compact and determined with their flame tails. Then I would lie down on my back watching them, hoping their engines wouldn't cut just then, hoping they would. I didn't want to get killed, but I wanted big explosions.

The days got hotter and hotter. The men still working on the rubble of the houses took their shirts off, and the bombs flew in a hard blue sky.

Just up the road from us stood a house rather larger than the rest. The Bellamies, who owned it, had moved to Wales at the start of the war, and let the house to some people called the Lorettis. I had hated them because everyone else did, and because their name was Italian. They had moved out a year before. When they went, the neighbours said, they had ripped all the electric wiring out of the walls.

Anyway, it was empty now, and the garden behind it a year overgrown. The Bellamies had said I could play there. It was the lawn which was so good; the grass was long enough to hide in, almost to get lost in. The flying bombs had made me forget this garden, but one stifling afternoon I suddenly thought of it, and went there to lie in the shade of the trees.

But that afternoon someone had got there before me. On the swing among the trees at the end of the garden was a girl. She was very sunburned, and was wearing a flowered summer dress. Red flowers on a white ground. I think it occurred to me that she was very pretty.

I went up to the swing. The girl looked younger than me, I was relieved to find. I stood there under the sun looking at her, wearing my grey steel helmet. I could feel the cramped sorbo lining damp with sweat against my forehead.

The girl stopped swinging and stared at me rather apprehensively.

'Mrs Bellamy said I could come here,' I said, in a tone which implied that the privilege was exclusive.

'Mrs Bellamy said *I* could come here, too,' replied the girl.

'I bet she didn't,' I said. It was the principle of the thing that worried me, not the girl. But though chivalry was a late addition to my character, I knew enough to know that you weren't supposed to hit girls, unless they were your sister. So I went back to the hot lawn and hid in the grass. I took off my helmet and tried to catch a grasshopper in it. Then I looked out to see if the girl had gone away. But she had just started swinging again.

After a while the siren went. Neither of us took any notice. I got tired of watching the girl swinging and wishing she would go away, and I could feel the sun burning my legs. Then, a long way away, there came the faint, uneven racket of a flying bomb. It got louder and louder till the bomb must have been almost overhead. The girl got off the swing, and started to walk uncertainly towards me, looking up at the sky. I stood up, to show I wasn't afraid. Suddenly the noise stopped.

'It's cut!' we both shouted. (This was a ritual.)

We threw ourselves down in the grass. There was a pause, which went on and on. The girl sneezed with the grass-pollen. I said 'Sh!' and the silence continued. The only sound was the whirring of the crickets. I started to say: 'It's probably . . .' when the explosion came, very satisfyingly loud.

'Less than half a mile away, I should think,' I said importantly.

'Aren't the doodlebugs fun?' said the girl.

'Our front door was blown off its hinges,' I boasted.

'Ours went right down the hall into the kitchen,' she replied. 'There was a lump of window-lead on my pillow next morning,' I said. 'It would have killed me if I hadn't been in the shelter.'

'I had a cut on my foot an inch deep from the glass,' she replied.

We went on exchanging details. I was pleased to find that I was a better liar than she was. Finally she stood up and said it was tea-time. She added:

'I expect you could come to tea with me if you liked.'

We left the overgrown garden, and crossed the road to her house. Her mother said yes, and we ran down the road to get my mother's permission.

We had tea in the kitchen, which was the coolest room in the house. Her mother had very white false teeth, and a face that was red from the sun. She laughed all the time as she ran about the kitchen making us cucumber sandwiches and took ice out of the refrigerator to put in our orangeade. I think I enjoyed the refrigerator best of all; we didn't have one.

'Alison,' said her mother, 'show Michael where the hot air comes from.'

'Feel on top,' Alison commanded me. I did so. 'You see, it's hot up there even though it's so cold inside.'

I nodded, trying to look clever.

'How does the refrigerator work?' I asked.

'It works on gas,' replied Alison solemnly.

It was certainly very strange.

One day the tilers arrived. They worked as a gang, and moved methodically from house to house up the street. One of them was a friendly young American called Mike. He always wore plimsolls, because he had bad feet. It was his bad feet that had kept him out of the army, he explained.

I was going through a stage of admiring the U.S.A., and I made Mike my hero simply because he was an American. (My other hero at this time was President Roosevelt.) But, as it happened, Mike filled the role very well. He was handsome, and he had the slow grin of a shy schoolboy. He ran up and down the ladders faster than the other tilers, and he walked over the steeply pitched loose Dutch tiles of the roofs as if he were on a dance-floor. Sometimes he would stand upright on the very pitch of the roof, his hands on his hips, grinning down at us like a monkey.

One morning, when the other tilers were drinking their eleven o'clock tea, Alison and I dragged Mike off to admire the Bellamies' garden.

'It's fine,' he said, looking round it happily. 'Bet you hope the war never ends.'

Alison and I threw ourselves down in the long grass. It was still wet with dew.

'You'll get yourselves soaked,' said Mike.

'It doesn't matter,' we said. He lay down beside us, plucked a blade of grass to chew, grinned and said: 'It's all right here, isn't it?'

We lay there in the fresh morning sunlight near the roses and enjoyed looking at one another. The left-hand pocket of Mike's ragged khaki shirt, over the heart, was embroidered with: Stella, Chicago, 1942.

'Who's Stella?' asked Alison. I had wanted to ask the same question, but had felt shy about it. Mike wasn't embarrassed, though. He just laughed and said:

'My sweetheart.'

I lay there in the wet grass, looking at him. Suddenly the sunlight seemed very sad. Mike in England, and Stella in Chicago. And Stella must be a very nice girl, I thought, if Mike likes her. Maybe the war wouldn't end for years, I thought, and for the first time I seriously wanted it to. But more than anything else I just felt a melancholy at the sadness of things.

'What about you two?' asked Mike, laughing again. 'Are you sweethearts?'

'Well . . .' I said, and blushed. It was a very surprising thought. I looked down at the droplets of dew on the grass.

F

I couldn't even breathe; my lungs were full of happiness. Maybe it was because 'sweetheart' was such a beautiful word. I looked through my fingers at Alison. She was smiling trustingly at Mike.

It was the best morning of the best summer since the start of the world.

'I'm going to put some more tiles on,' said Mike, getting up. 'Come and watch me run up that ladder.'

One day we went to the gardens of the bombed houses for a change. But there was something about those gardens, you couldn't feel at ease in them somehow. Besides, there was too much rubble lying around, and the gardens hadn't had time to get very overgrown yet.

But we did climb over the piles of rubble to see what we could find. We took a lot of objects home with us, but all I can remember now is a cut-glass decanter stopper, and the spout of an aluminium kettle. Someone else was picking over the site while we were there, too—a little old woman in a dirty trench-coat, who took away whatever it was she found in an old pram. She looked very furtive, and we felt furtive, too, doing the same thing.

The next day everyone was talking about the dreadful wave of bomb-site looting in the district. My father talked about the meanness of it over the evening spam-and-salad. People said that an old woman had been arrested on the other side of the village, pushing a whole pramful of stolen goods along. The police, they said, had orders to shoot looters on sight.

Alison and I hid the stopper and the spout and all the other things we had taken at the bottom of the Bellamies' garden. We were a bit ashamed of them now. But they were very beautiful.

Most mornings we used to watch the tilers. We told them that we were helping them. Mike said we did help them, too, and always thanked us.

But after lunch we would collect a pile of *Champions* and *Girls' Crystals* from an old trunk in Alison's summer-house, and take them over to the Bellamies' to read in the shade of the trees. Alison liked stories about fourth-formers foiling prefects who turned out to be German spies, while I liked detective stories. Sometimes we went back to Alison's for tea, and had ice-cubes from the refrigerator in our orangeade, and sometimes Alison's mother would give us fruit and sandwiches to take over to the Bellamies'. On the latter occasions Mike would bring his food over and join us. He never asked if we were sweethearts again. Sometimes, if we pestered him, he would tell us about America. At other times he would just prop himself up against the trunk of a tree and immerse himself in one of our comics. I never saw him read anything but the picture-strip stories on the cover, though.

After tea, when the air started to get a little cooler, we used to go on the swing. I initiated the practice of jumping off at the zenith of the swing's traverse. For a while it was quite exciting, and helped make up for the fact that there were fewer flying bombs coming over the district now. Alison was a bit afraid of this jumping game, though she wouldn't admit it, and when one day I insisted on trying a double jump, with her sitting and me standing, she cut her leg and ran home crying. I felt a bit guilty about it, and went home miserable myself. But she came to see me after dinner, so it was all right. And anyway, it was only a patch, not a bandage.

Another use we had for the garden was haymaking. We tore up grass by the handful and spread it out on the porch-step to dry, to make hay for Billy's bedding. Billy was Alison's rabbit, very old and pernickety. He didn't like anybody touching him except Alison. And Mike. Even Billy idolized Mike.

The days went by, each one seeming hotter than the last at noon, and more deliciously cool in the morning and evening. The grass in the Bellamies' garden started almost to dry out as it stood. It didn't seem as if a summer like that could ever end.

One afternoon, though, we had a thunderstorm. Bright, hard-edged clouds came up over the horizon after lunch, and by tea-time the whole sky was black. The air was intolerably close. When the storm broke about seven o'clock, the thunder cracked rather and rumbled, and it came almost on top of the lightning. I sat and watched the storm through the dining-room windows; it was more impressive than an air-raid. The rain hurled itself at the ground, fat drops streamlined into rods by their speed. It beat down the flowers, and churned the dry earth patches of the lawn into mud. I was shocked at its violence, and I could hear it still long after I had gone to bed.

But the next morning it was bright again, and the air was cool. I met two friends of mine on my way up the road to see Alison. They were on bicycles, but they got off with the eagerness of people who wanted an audience for exciting news.

'An Aircobra got struck by lightning last night,' said one of them.

'Got smashed to pieces,' said the other. 'It crashed on the Downs. It's super! We've just been to see it, and . . .'

'. . . and you know what?' broke in the other. 'The pilot got smashed to pieces too. We saw him! There was a finger caught in a tree . . .'

'. . . and I found one of his eyes on the ground.'

I rushed on to tell Alison the news, and we cycled up to the Downs at once. There was no difficulty about finding the remains of the plane; there was quite a crowd standing round it. I felt sick with a rather horrid kind of excitement, and at first neither of us dared look. When we did, however, there wasn't anything terrible to be seen; either the boys had been lying, or else someone had cleaned the place up.

But we took home a few pieces of camouflage-painted

aluminium, very jagged and twisted, and added it to the collection of shrapnel and grey flying bomb metal in my garage. We didn't tell Mike about this expedition, though: they said the pilot had been an American.

The weather was hot again. The ground dried out from the rain immediately, and we went back to the Bellamies' garden. We went on reading the *Champion*, cutting hay and drinking iced orangeade. We were both so brown now that it didn't matter how much we lay about in the sun.

Then one day, when we were on the swing, hidden by the trees, Mrs Dickenson climbed over the fence into the garden. Mrs Dickenson was the next-door neighbour. We didn't like her; for a start, although she was middle-aged, she had no children of her own. Also she dyed her hair, and smiled too much, and went to church too often, and was too good a neighbour to too many people. And now here she was, climbing into the garden—*our* garden. We watched her.

She started to pick in random haste all the ripe fruit she could lay her hands on—*our* fruit. We got off the swing and went over to stand behind her.

'Hullo, Mrs Dickenson,' said Alison. Mrs Dickenson dropped her basket and turned round. She gave us a sickening smile.

'Hullo,' she said at last; 'you startled me.'

We certainly had. Without another word or another apple she picked up her basket and climbed back over the fence. We watched her every yard of the way. She smiled again as she climbed down the other side.

Next morning we found the seat of the swing had been taken away. There was no doubt in our minds about who had done it, and we stormed away to demand justice.

We petitioned Alison's parents first of all. They refused nicely. Then we asked my parents. They not only refused to do anything, but said we had probably been making too much noise and had been disturbing Mrs Dickenson.

We were furious. We walked up and down in the Bellamies'
garden that evening, shouting at the top of our voices:

'Where's all the fruit gone?'

'Looks as if it's been pinched.'

'They're shooting looters on sight the other side of the
village.'

I remembered reading Cowper's 'Boadicea' at school. We
went back to my house and I copied it out in red ink, sub-
stituting 'Mrs Dickenson' for 'the Romans'. Then we put it in
Mrs Dickenson's letter-box and ran away, already very
frightened.

We heard next day that Mrs Dickenson had been to see the
father of a boy called Eric about this letter, and accused him,
in a roundabout, mincing way, of encouraging his son's ill
manners. Fortunately the man had thought she was mad, and
had thrown her out of the house instead of thrashing his son.

But the swing seat didn't reappear.

Billy died. We went to his cage one morning, and there he was,
dead. Alison cried for a long time, and wanted to stroke him,
but didn't dare. When Mike came he dug a grave at the top of
Alison's garden, and buried him. But Alison wouldn't cheer
up, and finally I got so miserable too that I went over to the
Bellamies' by myself. I picked up all the hay that was drying
in the porch to make poor Billy's bedding and hid it in the
tangled flower-beds, so that Alison shouldn't see it if she came
over. But she didn't come. I waited for a bit, and then went to
have a swing. But of course I couldn't.

Then Alison went away for a holiday with her family. I
missed her terribly. The track of the flying-bombs moved away
northwards, over London. Only an occasional stray one came
our way now. There wasn't much excitement left in life. Only
the weather held.

The tilers were due to leave the district, too. One afternoon
I watched them on their last house. I stood in our front-garden,

too miserable to go any nearer. The row of houses whose roofs they had patterned with clean tiles stretched up the road to this last house. And there they were, on the hot tiles. Mike was higher than the rest, standing on the very pitch of the roof, searching the sky for a flying-bomb they could hear. He stood there, very high and sharp and rich against the blue sky and the slow-moving summer cumulus which lay like a ceiling over the east.

I can remember this more clearly than anything else in the whole month.

I never saw Mike again. Alison is now the secretary of a hire-purchase company promoter. She's a very dull and stupid girl.

Those five people dead. All the best things in life are expensive, I think, whatever they say.

9 March 1957

Twin

ANDREW SINCLAIR

Pant upwards through the sloping moss-wood. Breath gulps and sweats inside you, bursts out, straining. Fling body on the long shelve of the grass that banks the stream. Face downwards, lips loose on the slithered green, suck air through the wet stems till the heart stills on the earth, till eyes look up towards the stream, bored with their blindness. See the blue dart flicker the arrowed air.

'Gosh, a kingfisher.'

'Where? Where?'

'It's gone now. Down along there.'

Point a finger down the course of the stream. Nothing now to show that quick passing. Only the stream, over-familiared with long-seeing.

'I can't see it.'

'It's gone.'

'Bet it wasn't there at all.'

'Bet it was.'

'Bet you a million it wasn't.'

'Bet you a trillion it was.'

'Bet you a trillion trillion it wasn't.'

Always the unending argument between the twins. Always Donald watching, knowing, leading; always James not seeing, not understanding, not believing. Two faces looking at each other, and seeing in each other only themselves. The difference is not mirrored between them.

They are tired now with inaction. They get up, and walk along the bank until they come to the ford and the stepping-stones. They leap across, balancing.

On the edge of the clearing they stop. Hunched over the fire of twigs on the three blackened stones is a boy, his back to them. He seems very square for a boy, not round and lumpy like their friend Fatso Anthony. He swivels his neck round to look at them, still squatting on his heels. His face is lined and brown, as old as the gardener's.

'Hello, kids,' he says.

He gets up, crookedly, and smiles. The boys stare at him and say nothing.

'My, my,' he says, 'you two are a couple of ones. Alike as two peas in a pod, and not a word between you.'

The boys still say nothing. He comes over to them.

'What's your names?' he says.

'I'm Donald. This is James.'

'Don and Jim. My name's Frank. I'm just having a cuppa. Come and have one with me.'

'Thank you, Mr Frank.'

'Frank. Just plain Frank.'

'Thank you, Frank.'

They sit around the fire. Frank asks Donald about his home. James sits, looking at him. His eyes never move. After a time, he speaks for the first time.

'Why are you so small?' he says.

Frank glances at him, side-long.

'I was born like that,' he says. 'I never growed.'

'Why?'

'I don't know. I just stopped growing.'

'I'd like always to be small,' Donald says. 'It must be stinky to be big. You couldn't get through the hole in the fence.'

'I want to be big,' James says.

'Don't always get what you want,' says Frank. 'Shall I show you how to make a proper fire?'

They are lost in the joy of a new knowledge until a sudden hunger finds their stomachs.

'Gosh, we're late,' Donald says. 'We must go to lunch.'

'Will you be here after?' James says.

'And teach us to make a real boat?'

'Maybe,' says Frank. 'How about you bringing me a little bit to eat?'

'I'm sure Mummy'll let us have something,' James says.

'Let's keep it a secret between us,' says Frank. He puts his finger to his throat and draws it across. 'Cross me throat. Swelp me God.'

The children imitate him.

'We won't tell,' Donald says.

'No,' James says.

They run back across the stream.

'We'll say we want a picnic tea,' Donald says. 'It's a fine day. Mummy won't mind.'

'Are you sure?'

'Course I am. I'll ask her if you're afraid.'

'I'm not afraid.'

'All right, you ask her then.'

'All right, I will.'

After lunch they nudge and shove each other. In the end Donald goes up to his mother, wheedling.

'Please, mummy, can we have a picnic tea? Please, mummy, just for today.'

'Don't forget to be in, then, in time for supper. Early bed tonight. Daddy and I want to go out.'

'Thank you, mummy.'

Donald smiles in triumph at James. James says:

'When are you taking us to the fair?'

'The day after tomorrow, if you're both good boys. No going before, mind. Promise me?'

'Yes,' the boys say together.

They go to the kitchen, and watch the cook cut them a

large tea, slicing through the bread delicately with a carving-knife. She makes a neat parcel of grease-proof paper, ties it with looped string. They run off with their prize, squabbling all the way to the clearing who shall give the parcel to Frank. Donald has done the work, Donald does the giving. Frank breaks the string with a quick jerk between his fingers like a shop-assistant. He eats the food in great gulps.

'God,' he says, 'that's good.'

He sleeps for much of the afternoon. The boat must wait until tomorrow. The boys play near him, trying to dam the stream. He wakes, and beckons them over to him.

'Going to the fair tonight?' he says.

James shakes his head.

'Mummy says we weren't to.'

'I never missed a fair when I was a kid.' He turns to Donald. 'You're going, Don, ain't you?'

'Yes,' Donald says. He sticks out his tongue at his brother.

'That's the boy.'

'I'm going too,' James says.

'Copycat,' Donald says.

'I'm not.'

'You are. Cowardy, cowardy, custard.'

'You're both a couple of real men,' says Frank. He feels in the pockets of his patched, incongruous grey flannels. 'You'll do something for me, Don, won't you? Write me a letter.'

He pulls a stub of pencil and a dirty page of paper out of his pocket. Donald lies proudly on his stomach on the ground, resting the paper on the stone of the fire, now gone out.

'What can I do?' James says.

'Go and help Don.'

Frank looks up at the sky. He picks his nose. James stares jealously over Donald's shoulder.

'Dear Gloria,' says Frank. He pauses. 'I love you. Jim don't mean nothing. He'll do you dirt soon as he can. Can't we be as we was. Honest. I'm giving it to you straight. Love. Tich.'

'But your name's Frank.'

'Not to them. Let's have a dekko.'

He takes the paper Donald holds out to him. He pretends to read it.

'Very nice,' he says. 'Now, kiddo, I want you to take it along to the fair tonight. Ask any of the boys. Just say, I've got a letter for Gloria. And give it to her. And tell me what she says. Got it. A letter for Gloria. And come back and tell me.'

'I'll go too,' James says.

Donald says:

'I'll manage it, Frank.'

'You're a pal,' says Frank.

When they are walking slowly home to supper, James says to his brother:

'Mummy did tell us not to.'

'Funk,' Donald says. 'She'll never find out.'

II

Stay awake, eyes half-closed in the half-dark. Wait till the sound of the front door slammed. Then up, soles cold on the carpet, across to the window, and watch the car creep out along the drive, hesitate at the gate, swing left, faster, faster, down the road. Back to the chair where your clothes are folded. Put them on, fumbling the buttons, leaving the shoe-laces undone. A whisper from the bed.

'Donald, you're not going.'

'Shut up.'

Slowly to the door, slowly turn the handle, slowly down the stairs, god, how slowly, pausing at each creak. Slowly to the main door, slowly twist the Yale-lock, click, and the catch is fast and the door shut-to behind you and you're away and free and running, running through the warm dark.

The sound of the fair and people going towards it you meet a long way away. Squeeze in through the hole in the hedge, and you're among it all, all of it, the lights bright as fired pennies, the glare and the wheel and the harsh and the loud of the voices, begging voices, bellowing voices, voices that bang into your ear, near voices, far voices. And round and round and round the merry-go-round and roundabout, arching, flying, dying on the circle of the world, till there's a nothing in your pocket and a nothing in your stomach and an ache in your head. Then remember in the lurch of quick panic why you're here, why you're not in bed, what if your father finds out. Go up to the woman who smiles from the stall, holding three wooden balls in her hand. Hold up the crumpled piece of paper. Say:

'I've got a letter for Gloria.'

'Have you, ducks? You'll find her back over there.'

She points to a booth where a crowd clusters. Donald walks across. On the blaring signs he reads—BLOOM'S MIDGET MIMICS —THE SMALLEST MAN IN THE WORLD—then in smaller letters— Gorgeous Gloria. The Pint-sized Poppet. Donald goes to the back of the tent. He trips over a guy-rope. As he picks himself up, there is a giggle in the smothered shadows. Donald says:

'Please, I've got a letter for Gloria.'

'That's me,' says a high voice. 'Who's it from?'

'Frank.'

'He means Tich,' says a deep voice from beside the high voice. 'Cor, that's rich.'

A small old-faced girl flounces out of the shadow, her hair over-blonde in tight curls, dressed in white, creased, sequinned lace.

'Let's see,' she says. She reads the note. She laughs, shrill as a breaking wire. 'He wants to come back,' she says. 'Bloody cheek. Got a pencil, Jim?'

A tall man comes from the shadows.

'Why can't he do his own dirty work, see? You tell him I'll do him if he shoves his dirty nose in again.' He gives her a pencil.

She squats on her heels, supporting the paper on her knee. She presses some letters on to the paper. She rises.

'Here,' she says, 'take this. And tell him Jim'll do him if he pokes his nose around here.'

Donald goes away to the noise of laughter behind him, the high voice and the low voice in cackled dissonance behind him. He pushes his way through the legs and the bodies of the fair, until he's on the road, dragging his toes home. The car head-lights pin him against the dark, hold him as the brakes screech.

'Donald,' says his mother, 'what are you doing here? Have you been to the fair?'

He says nothing, but climbs in through the open car-door on to his mother's knee.

'We'll talk about it in the morning,' his father says. 'You'll be kept in bed till I get back from work.'

'Naughty boy,' his mother says.

Donald dozes, his fist clenched in his pocket on the letter.

III

James and Donald wake as their mother comes into the room.

'Get up, James,' she says. 'Donald, you're to stay in bed till your father gets home this evening.'

'But, mummy . . .'

'No questions. You'll do as you're told. Come on, James. Breakfast's spoiling.'

She goes out of the door.

'Did they catch you?' James says, dressing.

'Yes.'

'What shall I tell Frank?'

'I'll tell him.'

'You can't. You're in bed. He might be gone by tomorrow morning.'

Donald bites his lip.

'Tell him Jim'll do him if he goes round there. And the letter's in my pocket.'

James goes across the room, and takes the letter out of Donald's trousers. He goes to the door.

'You will tell Frank it was me?' Donald says.

'Yes.'

James runs through the wood, over the stones of the stream. Frank is lying by the fire.

'Hello, kiddo,' he says. 'Where's Don?'

'He can't come. I got something for you. Jim'll do you if you go back. And this.' He gives Frank the paper, now dirty as a handkerchief.

Frank untwists the paper.

'What does it say?'

James reads the large, mis-shapen letters. Five letters. One word.

'Freak. Just freak.'

'Oh god,' says Frank. He puts his face in his hands.

'I don't mind,' says James.

'Thanks, kiddo,' Frank says. He gets up. 'Time I went.' He begins collecting together his bundle. James watches him.

'Good-bye, kiddo,' he says. 'Say good-bye to Don for me.'

James looks at him going, a dwarf, through the thinning trees.

As he walks home, he sees the kingfisher, perched on a twig. He watches it for a full minute before it flies down the stream. He has seen, and Donald is not there.

26 November 1955

Gouda

CHRISTOPHER LEVENSON

Between high walls, like spiders, in the courtyard
The old men gossip, waiting for the summer
Enviously, like tottering houses propped
Upon their sticks and crutches,
And while on the canal the mild winds ferry
A lately severed leaf over the weir,
Lost behind quiet alleys
The bald head of a watchmaker bends to his work,
The great church strikes, flexing twigs at his window
Shadow him, mark time across his brow.

The houses stifle in lace.

4 May 1957

E. M. Forster

TIMOTHY BIRDSALL

timothy
1958

24 January 1959

E. M. Forster

JONATHAN SPENCE

'The man, as he should be, is alive and with a tendency to smile.'

HEMINGWAY

E. M. Forster's scale of values is apparently so simple and so attractive that it is in constant danger of over-simplification or misrepresentation. He is associated comfortably with liberalism, humanism and belief in personal relations; he maintains a sympathetic if distant interest in progressive movements; he continues to speak up for tolerance, courage and gaiety; he is a friendly and courteous author whom Holden Caulfield would almost certainly want to call up on the telephone. This impression Forster in person does nothing to qualify. Recent interviews have shown him genial, worried, amusing, interested in his own characters as human beings but strangely silent about their wider implications. The reason for this reticence may be his modesty and engaging self-depreciation, it may be his lifelong dislike of talking big, evidenced in the chatty and colloquial style which he sometimes adopts. More important are his hints at the limitations of the novel as a vehicle of truth; he is capable of irreverence towards other novelists' technical feats, as with Gide, of whose *The Counterfeiters* he writes: 'he is indeed a little more solemn than an author should be about the whole caboodle'. Then there are the deprecatory remarks about 'this low atavistic form' in

Aspects of the Novel, he has a 'reservation about this prophetic stuff', and both he and Rickie Elliot hanker after the
perfection of statement that music can bring.

On the other hand this chattiness and depreciation does not
prevent his engagement with the largest issues: 'Though I am
not an optimist, I cannot agree with Sophocles that it were
better never to have been born. And although, like Horace, I
see no evidence that each batch of births is superior to the last,
I leave the field open for the more complacent view. This is
such a difficult time to live in, one cannot help getting gloomy
and also a bit rattled, and perhaps short sighted.' And there is
tremendous spiritual arrogance behind the phrase 'poor little
talkative Christianity'. The seriousness *is* there, and in face of
the apparent self-disparagement it is necessary to emphasise
that his achievement in the five novels was something more
difficult and more momentous than he would have us believe.

In Forster's earliest work his later ideas and themes are
present, but the issues are simplified and the treatment is that
of fantasy rather than prophecy. The characters are neatly
marshalled, the author's preferences and prejudices are obvious. In the most effective of the short stories, *The Road to
Colonus* and *The Machine Stops*, as in *Where Angels Fear to
Tread* and *A Room with a View*, nearly every character can
be typed by a quotation. There are changes, Philip 'undergoes
conversion', Lucy 'enters the army of the benighted' and is
rescued, but on the whole, as George Emerson remarks, 'men
fall into two classes—those who forget views and those who
remember them even in small rooms'. The battle is between
those of broadness of vision and those without, between those
who understand nature and those incapable of so doing,
between those who see life whole and those whose lives are
bounded by 'petty unselfishness'. Southern sun and vitality
meet and triumph over northern fog and hypocrisy in a
world in which 'a Gothic statue implies celibacy just as a
Greek statue implies fruition'. For such a simple statement of

the problem a simple solution is adequate and this, with much humour and technical skill, Forster supplies.

But in *The Longest Journey* and *Howards End* this same neatness of solution is retained, while Forster's treatment of his characters and their predicament has developed in breadth and complexity. His description of, and attitude towards, the benighted remains constant, as he has summarised it in a much quoted passage from *Abinger Harvest*:

'And they go forth into a world that is not entirely composed of public-school men or even of Anglo-Saxons, but of men who are as various as the sands of the sea; into a world of whose richness and subtlety they have no conception. They go forth into it with well-developed hearts . . . An undeveloped heart—not a cold one. The difference is important.' Herbert Pembroke, Agnes and the Wilcoxes are at home here, but for their opponents a simple denial is no longer sufficient. Rickie not only has to fight against absorption into the values of Sawston; he has to face the consequences of his own gentle confusion. Warned against trying to love everyone equally, he is still unable to distinguish reality in people or their actions; and even after escape from Sawston he cannot see clearly and is let down once again. He takes death when it comes 'wearily', losing the world without gaining his own soul. *The Longest Journey* shows Forster's development in two ways: his realisation that a balanced life on this earth is not the simple triumph of white over black as he at first pictured it, that the problem is not one of good and evil but of 'good-and-evil': and a growing understanding of the novelist's ability as commentator to place the characters in a wider context, using broader, underlying rhythms and 'echoes' (Orion, the level-crossing, the Rings) a process reaching perfection in *A Passage to India*.

On a different level it is this technique that Forster uses to achieve his humorous effects. His characters very rarely make funny remarks or get into ludicrous situations; the humour comes from Forster's comments on their thoughts and actions: 'Then (Stephen) went to harness the horse, while Mr Pembroke, watching his broad back, desired to bury a knife in it. The desire passed, partly because it was unclerical, partly because he had no knife, and partly because he soon blurred over what had happened.' This quotation reminds one that Forster has the talent that he ascribes to Virginia Woolf: 'though most of us like to write sometimes seriously and sometimes in fun, few of us can so manage the two impulses that they speed each other up, as hers did'. For the second idea is straight comedy, but the first is a caustic comment on Pembroke's pompous and hypocritical attitude to life, while the third is a crucial view of Forster's which he further emphasises in *Howards End*. 'The anodyne of muddledom, by which most men blur and blend their mistakes, never passed Leonard's lips—

> And if I drink oblivion of a day
> So shorten I the stature of my soul.

It is a hard saying, and a hard man wrote it, but it lies at the foot of all character.'

The Longest Journey ends with the withdrawal of Stephen into a world of nature in which he can be sure of his own values. Nature for Forster is no longer an ideal from the Mediterranean world, but is specifically identified with the countryside of England, with the Roman Rings and the hills of Wiltshire, with the earth on which Stephen sleeps with his child while the whistle of Herbert's Pembroke's train fades into the distance. *Howards End* is also concerned with England and, allegorically, with the struggle of different classes for its soil. But as Stephen's entry into his heritage seems an inadequate compensation for the sufferings of Rickie and the stupidity of Pembroke, so the final scene of *Howards End*, when Margaret tells Henry that 'nothing has been done wrong', and the child of Leonard and Helen plays in the meadow, seems too neat. Even if the study of Schlegels and Wilcoxes, their inter-relation, the confrontation of 'a civilisation of luggage' with 'a civilisation that won't be a movement because it will rest on the earth' are wonderfully handled, is there here a realisation of Margaret's desire to 'connect the prose and the passion' or an assurance that Helen's 'panic and emptiness' may not return? Should not the Schlegels come to terms with the world within the world itself, living out their values in continued conflict if necessary? And if 'it is fair to say that the book's value is in the definition rather than in the problem' (Rex Warner) there is a further criticism —that Forster is limited by his social and intellectual ties; and his brilliance within the range of his experience accentuates the fact that he is not equipped to deal either with material privation or with class suffering. It is not merely that ironically 'we are not concerned with the very poor. They are unthinkable, and only to be approached by the statistician or the poet', but that Leonard Bast who stands just above this gulf is not convincingly realised; and that Forster's voice is here the voice he attributes to Ruskin : 'full of high purpose, full of beauty, full even of sympathy and the love of men, yet somehow eluding all that was actual and insistent in Leonard's life. For it was the voice of one who had never been dirty or hungry, and had not guessed successfully what dirt and hunger are.'

In *Howards End* Forster attempts a reconciliation between the 'inner life', and 'the world of telegrams and anger' whose panic and emptiness is sensed behind its bustle and decision. In *A Passage to India* he re-examines his values in a context of universal significance and extent. As James McConkey says in *The Novels of E. M. Forster*, this novel is the expression of a double vision, a human reality and a transcendent world. Forster's position is mediatory between the two realms, attempting to reconcile them; his characteristic tone of voice is one of compassion and love purchased at the cost of detachment, withdrawal and abnegation of individual desire. Thus McConkey sees in Godbole, the mystic, the final expression of Forster's 'prophetic voice'; Godbole who is aware of his spiritual unity with the wasp and Mrs Moore, who says: 'Good and evil are different as their names imply. But, in my own humble opinion, they are both of them aspects of my Lord. He is present in the one, absent in the other, and the difference between presence and absence is great, as great as my feeble mind can grasp. Yet absence implies presence, absence is not non-existence, and we are therefore entitled to repeat, "Come, come, come, come".' *A Passage to India* is Forster's last novel because in it he has put down all he can know; as Peter Burra writes echoing Forster's own words, 'the organism, being perfectly adjusted, is silent'.

But McConkey in fact emphasises only one segment of Forster's vision, and the greatness of *A Passage to India* lies in the novelist's comprehensiveness, his awareness of the delicate gradations within the English and Indian societies, and of the complexity of levels between the human and the transcendent common to both. Between the void of weariness and meaninglessness which Mrs Moore enters, in which 'everything exists, nothing has value'—the negative vision which is nightmare— and the mystical vision of Godbole which is harmony, falls the decent and prosaic world of Adela and Ronny, Fielding and Aziz, in which a measure of stability can be and is sustained, despite the inevitable failures of communication and transient disasters. It is of this latter world that Forster says in *What I Believe*, 'not by becoming better, but by ordering and distributing his native goodness, will Man shut up Force into its box, and so gain time to explore the universe and to set his mark upon it worthily'. The possibilities of failure here Forster has often admitted. In *A Passage to India* he shows most clearly the possibilities of a measured success, of an existence in which life may remain a mystery but need not be a muddle, where we may perhaps perceive 'the horror of the universe and its smallness' without losing a sense of its harmony and its sanity, or of the reality of those things we have learnt to value. We may gain a 'sense of deities reconciled' as in the other novels, but now with an added grandeur; because the deities are larger and more powerful than we had suspected and yet their reconciliation, though arduous and dangerous, is not beyond man's power.

24 January 1959

The Dove Breeder

TED HUGHES

Love struck into his life
Like a hawk into a dovecote.
What a cry went up!
Every gentle pedigree dove
Blindly clattered and beat,
And the mild-mannered dove-breeder
Shrieked at that raider.

He might well wring his hands
And let his tears drop:
He will win no more prizes
With fantails and pouters,
(After all these years
Through third, up through second places
Till they were all world beaters. . . .)

Yet he soon dried his tears

Now he rides the morning mist
With a big-eyed hawk on his fist.

18 May 1957

Resolve

SYLVIA PLATH

day of mist : day of tarnish

with hands
unserviceable, I wait
for the milk van.

the one-eared cat
laps its grey paw

and the coal fire burns

outside, the little hedge leaves are
become quite yellow.
a milk-film blurs
the empty bottles on the windowsill.

no glory descends.

two water drops poise
on the arched green
stem of my neighbor's rose bush

o bent bow of thorns.

the cat unsheathes its claws
the world turns.

today
today I will not
disenchant my twelve black-gowned
                         examiners
or bunch my fist
in the wind's sneer.

9 March 1957

The Fantastic Case of the Widow Speake

PETER COOK

News of the Widow's arrest came filtering through to the public via Mr P. K. Prill, a lonely man of 9 The Parade, Gorlsdon. How he came by it is an open secret in the region, and Prill, or Bingham as he is sometimes called, is not widely liked. None the less not even Herr Stanger would deny that it was via him that the facts of the Speake case came filtering through.

Had he actually seen the rough law-men bundle the startled Widow into the Black Maria or was he merely retailing tittle tattle that had leaked out of the Yard? How first-hand his details were is reasonably uncertain and now that Inspector Tollit has imposed an official gag it seems unlikely that the German-born but well-loved Herr Stanger will ever pierce the Prill façade. Not until a government decides to rip away the veils that smother this case will the Widow's ordeal be bathed in its true light.

This much is known. The Widow Speake is a woman of spritely charm who suffers fools lightly; but tyranny has never been welcome in her house and she would have sharp words for men who tried to strike her down with sticks. 'I'd rather be stung by a bee than be poisoned to death by foreigners' is one remark that could often be heard about her living room. (And a more spick and span little room could scarcely be imagined; one may rest assured that it was not on account of untidiness that she was arrested.) Mr Speake, a shadowy figure, did not live to see his wife in custody and it must be admitted that the manner of his death may have influenced Inspector Tollit and his cronies in the Force. Was it the ravages of old age that had left him so dead on the settee or had he passed on for other reasons? Why for instance did the Widow at once set about achieving the marriage rites for a second time instead of moping in her weeds? These questions must surely have weighed heavily on the minds of the Police and it is probable that the rich G. N. Arles, at whom the Widow was levelling her now eligible charms, was behind the moves that led to her sudden detention.

At the station a burly constable worked the plucky woman over, hoping to extract statements that would win him his long due promotion; but the Widow stood firm and later the foiled man was to describe her as 'a clam'. For days she bided her time in her cell and only then did she first take legal bearings; her skilled barristers agreed with her that the case was by no means won and that pessimism was the order of the day. 'I dare say you'll hang,' cried one adept man. Her defence was to be based mainly on points of order and here it was hoped that her erstwhile friends in Leeds might play a vital role in swinging the trend in her favour. But they had not reckoned with a biased judge and a jury that was to sow unease throughout the court.

The hearing was to be heard on a Thursday, a date ill-suited to the plans she had bruited abroad to the press. At once there was confusion in the court as the noble Widow, dressed and as pretty as some pictures, strode into the box. Hammers swung and order returned; now she felt that the crowd were on her side and her gestures were confident at this stage. All was soon under way and the prosecution sprang witness after witness upon the surprised but plucky Widow.

'Where were you?' shouted the bluff prosecuting counsel.

The Widow moaned.

'Answer me yes or no,' the unperturbed man droned on.

'Get out!' was the Widow's firm retort.

Tumult in the court; the anti-Speake factions rumbled nastily. The third-rate judge became alarmed and sought an adjournment but still the case swept on.

'How old were you at the time?'

No answer from the Widow; was she nonplussed or playing for sympathy?

'Answer me Widow, speak!'

Further tumult in the court with cries of 'Widow, speak!' and 'Widow Speake!' Yet another group of partisans were shouting 'Speak Widow Speake!' Confusion was rife and the jury showed every sign of bias.

It was then that the defence roped in an element of surprise by calling for the Widow's Peke. At first this was thought to be a jest to enable the Widow to recover her aplomb; but no, the tiny creature did exist and was brought on in the cupped hands of a worried official. The peke had not seen the crime and this was hailed as conclusive by the overconfident defence. The Widow sighed and relief seemed to be stamped on her face; but it was here that events took a grim turn as the lively prosecuting counsel made several disparaging remarks about her widow's peak.

At the mention of her hair the Widow blanched and there was further hubbub in the panelled court while flash-bulbs exploded and noise reared its ugly head.

'Order in the court!' cried the man in charge, but still the sounds were rife; once again the paltry judge tried to muster an adjournment to no real avail; meanwhile the peke had evaded its caretaker and was scuttling here and there on the floor, the tiny paws flailing, the tiny jaws working. 'Trap the Widow's peke' was one cry that could be distinguished.

In the disorder that followed the versatile Widow was able

to adopt one of her incredible disguises and began to move among the jury unobserved, prejudicing them in her favour. The Clerk of the Court was suddenly aware of her absence and felt fairly embarrassed as the case would fold up without her.

'Widow Speakes!' was the anxious call of a man with a wretched memory for names.

And yet the Widow took little heed and continued to circulate, spreading her own very personal kind of propaganda. But here again the hand of fate stepped in and provided what has been called 'the turning point in the fantastic saga'. Already the jury were swinging towards her and the judge too seemed less hostile than of wont, but the anti-Speake factions were stronger than one person at least had suspected.

'To the lanterns with her!' screamed these biased people. 'Hanging the Widow Speake is what we're in favour of!' And no amount of skilled defence could quell their noisy interpolations.

The tawdry judge was of course put out and the prosecuting counsel, angered at the Widow's fleet evasions, were in no mood for trifling. Still the Widow moved amongst the jury, but they too were tiring of her disguise and whispering of a hostile nature was bandied about.

'Retire!' screamed the gimcrack judge.

'Guilty is the verdict you should hit upon,' said N. J. Nind for the prosecution.

The Widow beamed and adopted another disguise. Useless.

'Even to us she seems nearer to guilty than innocent,' opined her futile defence.

'To the lanterns, the Widow hanging from the lanterns is the sight we want to see!' raved the rabble in unison.

And so this amazing case drew to a biased close. Conviction set in and the brave Widow has been detained. Whatever our personal opinions of her merits or sins we must stand back and admire her pluck. Over this Herr Stanger and Mr Prill are in agreement. G. N. Arles has probably not heard the last of the Widow Speake and few will deny that it is only right that she should be appealing.

6 June 1959

da capo

WILLIAM DUNLOP

Barred from the garden, made to scrub my hands,
Sulky, but not yet prompted to rebel,
My straining fingers half an octave spanned.
Father, seduced by feminine persuasion,
Had paid my fees, installed a Baby Grand.

Yet, wise in my predestined generation
(Promised an apple if I practised well)
I glimpsed the serpent in the treble clef,
Unlike my mother, grasped the implication,
Read his contorted signature aright;
Born to this conflict forking black and white.

Initial bars, though sharp with overtone,
Engaged no accidental quest:
Five fingers yearning bone to bone,
My heart a faltering metronome,
Bone of my bone I struck, depressed.

I modulate from stage to stage,
Pounding by treadmill scales to death—
My erring parents taxed my breath
Mortgaged my garden heritage.

8 March 1958

G

Three Cartoons

JONATHAN MILLER

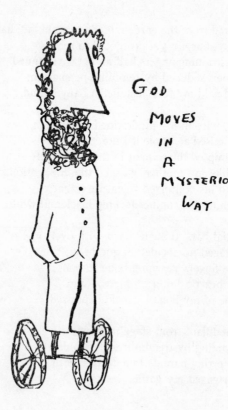

GOD
MOVES
IN
A
MYSTERIOUS
WAY

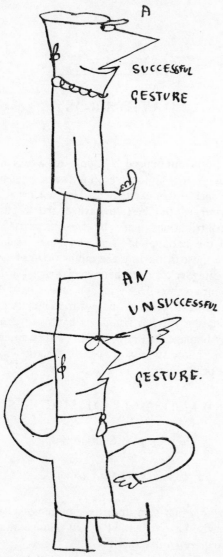

8 June 1954

Free Enterprise

DAVID FROST

The competition announced a couple of weeks ago in the *World's Press News*—for articles in praise of free enterprise—has raised considerable excitement. The first prize is of £500 for the writer of the best 'published article showing the beneficial contributions made by free-enterprise trade and industry to the national life and economy'. *Granta* editors however are most thrilled by the minor prize of £100 in the 'magazine category', since there is a crucial rider to the announcement to the effect that 'journalists or their editors' can submit material. Always anxious to stimulate integrity in all its fascinating variety, *Granta* is happy to print its first spontaneous homage to the principle of free enterprise. We will of course allow successful authors the customary 10 per cent. of the prize money.

SWEET SMELL OF SUCCESS

The Man who Built an Empire

EXPRESS STAFF REPORTER

There are words that sum up in two or three syllables what might otherwise have taken five or ten minutes to say.
And there are men like that too.

If the subject is free enterprise then bluff Lancashire ex-mill-owner, Frederick Black, is just such a man.

Shrewd ('I've never had to pay a fair price yet') and outspoken ('Got no time for all this pensions nonsense') his wealth was built on the great Frederick Black Hook-and-Eye Empire.

When he came on the scene at the age of 28, there were five hook-and-eye firms all in competition with each other. Eight years later there was one.

'God helps those who help themselves,' he often recalls.

His whole career has been founded on this simple philosophy of life. A Calvinist, he has never had much time for the inefficiently-run business concern—as many have found to their cost.

HUTS

By 1948, Frederick Black was the biggest hook-and-eye manufacturer this side of the Iron Curtain. Then came his masterstroke.

He noted that it would not be long before the Army required more sheet-constructed huts. He saw also that there were only two potential suppliers left in the country. He seized his opportunity, and switched his whole factory over to hut construction.

'A man of steel,' the newspapers called him, for in those days of troubled labour relations any move involving the immediate redundancy of more than 500 men required considerable courage.

His enemies attempted to make capital out of the situation, but he still went ahead. He has often said since how much he resented the unwelcome publicity.

Within six months the Black Factory was in full production. Now he was ready to proceed. First he approached the other two firms, and suggested that they meet all Government hut enquiries with a joint front.

Black's offer of friendship failed, and he was forced to resort to other methods. Soon both firms became more co-operative and when an urgent Government order for 500 huts for camps abroad was received, it was Black who led the delegation to the Ministry.

He demanded orders for 2,000 huts, or there was, as he put it, 'nothing doing'.

'I have friends on both sides of the House,' he warned, but the Ministry acted on impulse and refused his offer. It was not until six months later that news of the hardship their indecisive policy was causing abroad forced the Ministry to adopt a more reasonable attitude towards Black's demands.

Black's patient policy had its reward. The huts were ordered and delivered. After all their foreign needs had been met, the Ministry set about the disposal of the remaining 1,500 huts—by building 'ghost' camps—'a Russian invasion will find us well prepared,' Black told me—and by periodic sales up and down the country at which many churches and chapels have found bargains that must have saved them hundreds of pounds.

REWARDS

But this is nothing compared with the difference these moves made to the already prosperous Black Empire. Black is rich. He has no illusions about that.

'I'm trying to rid life of its illusions,' he has often said.

He knows too that his rewards have been far greater than those of his colleagues.

'You will never equate life and justice,' he told me simply on one occasion. 'With the world as imperfect as it is, wealth will always be concentrated in a few hands. And what will happen to our freedom if anyone starts trying to make changes?

'Freedom is all too precious a gift for us to imagine it will cost us nothing. We must expect to suffer a little injustice and a little inequality, a little hardship and a little misery as the price of our freedom. For,' he warned, 'if we lose our freedom, we lose our souls.'

And if that's what free enterprise means to a man who has seen so much of it, then surely that's what it ought to mean to us.

7 March 1959

HE SAID
HIS NAME
WAS
GRENDEL

Cortège

ALEXIS LYKIARD

Permissible
to take life from the dead?
these stately black slugs
& their garish flowers
slide past with luck
for all who are not dead

cars chew the cemetery gravel
& the expectant hands of the dead
writhe up from under the graves
like white flowers, voracious

Machines bearing a box
              bearing a man
the smell of petrol dissolves the smell
of death—
the flower in my lapel,
partaking of both odours,
transcends both

January 1962

Snowing

ANON.

We are privileged to bring readers, in advance of publication, this excerpt from the latest volume in the autobiography of the eminent autobiographer Mr Leonard Foxx. We have already obtained an option on Mr Foxx's forthcoming volumes, provisionally titled Owing, Hoeing, Towing *and* Crowing. *The compendious work* Knowing *will, we are sure, be a landmark in the history of autobiography. We are looking for a suitable reviewer.*

About this time I remember going with Vanessa, Maynard and one or two others (among whom was a short, incredibly stupid man of 35 called Crayston—or some such name— whom Lytton for obscure reasons had taken up) to a performance given by Njinsky in East Dulwich. We hired a cab afterwards but, overcome by a sort of cosmic loneliness that often invaded us at that time, paid off the driver and took to walking under the opaque velvety sky. The occasion is very clear to me, painful as it was, owing to a rather unpleasant rash I had developed on the scrotum. Clive, whose presence earlier on in the evening I did not recall, began a conversation on transcendentalism in his usual pellucid and eloquent style. Vanessa and I responded avidly. Of course Crayston, if that was his name, was far too dull a dog to have anything of interest to say, but we were in a benevolent mood under the stimulation of the superb dancing, and treated his utterances

G*

with huge indulgence. Although I have been a socialist since approaching my sixth birthday in April 1887, I have never fallen into the gross heresy of imputing intelligence to the dunces of mankind. There is a little Provençal lyric Vanessa once embroidered on a sampler for Tom which sums up the indefeasible nullity of the masses as moral, political and social agents more competently than I now feel able to do. I would reproduce it had the sampler not been accidentally included in a make-do-and-mend bundle we gave to Stephen Spender when we moved from Tavistock Square during the latter half of 1943.

While we were crossing Hungerford Bridge, I remarked on the slipshod geometry (a phrase I actually used, as I recall) of the stars and the inconceivable nature of any patterning in the universe. At this time, devout people still used to pretend that they discerned some kind of order in life. Adrian once told me that when he came down from Magdalene, which through some oversight he had had to enter as a commoner, and came up to London to meet the intellectual society we moved in, it was as if he had stepped into technicolor from a monochrome film. Such was the gap at this juncture between the ordinary hidebound conventionalists who still dominated the great offices of church and state, and the free spirits in the rationalist camp. Desmond took up my remarks with enthusiasm. He had been conversing brilliantly about Emerson as we watched the twinkling lights of Southwark recede. Some time afterwards, at a house party in Rye in 1927, he told me that he had not in fact read Emerson, but I still treasure his dazzling exposure of the American's pretensions as we crossed the dear and familiar footbridge. . . .

I have described in an earlier chapter how I first committed sodomy in Saigon in 1908. It will be recalled how J. N. Darellcourt, later Sir Jerome Darellcourt, High Commissioner for Borneo, introduced me to homosexual practices. With the openmindedness which characterised all my doings at this period, I retained a tolerant interest in the subject even after my marriage and my resumption of badminton. On one occasion I made rather a good joke on the point to Roger Fry. Unfortunately I cannot recall the exact terms, and in any case it would suffer with the telling.

However, my violent opposition to the admission within our *cénacle* of the notorious Tinkie Treadmont demands explanation at this stage. I believe it my duty as an auto-biographer to record all details of my life, however compromising. I now consider, in this instance, that I acted wrongly towards Treadmont, and that my behaviour was nasty, calculated, snobbish, cowardly and vile. This is partly attributable to certain unfortunate experiences I had at the hands of Treadmont's second cousin during my fourth term at St Paul's. Even so, I must frankly avouch to the reader that in later years I have not been altogether happy about the part I played in getting Treadmont fifteen years' penal servitude.

I do not perfectly recollect all the details of the case, which became known to our group thanks to Lytton's witticism as the 'Et ego in Burlington Arcadia' affair. Luckily it happens that I am able to supplement my memory, defective as it is in two or three immaterial points, with letters on the subject which I chanced to address to Moore, Lytton, Vanessa, Roger and T. M. Paulsby (later Fellow of All Souls', and the husband of the under-rated poetess Eustacia Paulsby, connected on her father's side with Shelley as well as the Cornfords). I will quote first from the letter I wrote to Moore who was at that time in Lossiemouth . . .

April 1962

A Continuum

TOM LOWENSTEIN

Removed, it would thrive
in any place or climate,
unfavoured by the chances
of contact, or the poison
of deliberate encounters.

It would take root
on any stone—or under it
would grow, grow white,
live under a stone,
with no reservations.

And then a flash—
a match or the gas,
would show for a moment,
by means of contrast,
what darkness it endured.

It would live on,
this mortality,
like memory
on the mind.
It is a piece of life

hardly worth living:
for the amnesia,
the moments we have mislaid
thankfully,
exist invisibly—

even the heart's
exhausted thunder
timed to be extinguished
unexpectedly,
thuds on.

19 October 1963

Colony

TERRY EAGLETON

At noon we watch the air explode the trees
to their ingredients, twig, leaf—and freeze,
straining each nerve, a wild growth of shapes
whole on the eyeball till the image breaks
spawning at touch and slides across the sand.
We hear the gristle singe beneath the tanned
bone, scorch to rubber, watch the boulders rust
away, crack with a fury we can't thrust
aside or strain to mirage with a stare.
The native children flout us. We are here
to weld the spawning fragments of their lives
to postures noon rejects, for now white hives
of sweat return all posture to its raw
ingredients: the children's bodies blur
slowly like leaves into the thrashing air.

19 October 1963

•

The Midget Wrestlers

PAT ROGERS

Student reformist pressure is a hard thing to write about. It invites from senior members either the quick dismissive shrug or else an amiable and distant patronage. Most of them, I think, are aware of this pressure as a vague buzzing in the ears—a sound at once insistent and near-hysterical, urgent yet monotonous, like the girlie noises back of a Tamla-Motown disc. Not that the Colleges pay too little attention. On the contrary, they are perhaps over-solicitous. The most hastily trumped up undergraduate memorandum will be gravely circulated, as though it were a round robin for a super-annuated functionary whom everyone respected but no-one quite liked. The Master will add small ticks and queries in the margin, whilst the Senior Tutor will append his initials to the sixty-eighth paper to reach him that day. All very well, you say, but nothing will get done. This is true in most cases; and it's my aim here to suggest some reasons why that might be so. In sketching out the main lines of a case that usually goes by default, one risks appearing arrogant, complacent or snob-bish. I think the risk is well worth taking, if it means achiev-ing more honesty than usual on this subject.

Two provisos. The structure of this article will be one of rather devious arrangement, which is a polite way of saying it will be broken-backed. I shall be veering about from a few particular quarrels to a general case about the nature and function of a University education. This is the merest wash of

inductive method spread over what I have to say; and the
case won't stand or fall by its adequacy. Secondly, I am talking about education in the humanities. Those of us trained in
this field don't know clearly enough what sort of activity
scientific enquiry is to make any sensible comment. We see
the results, observe the methods, contemplate the world view;
but by definition you have to be a scientist to assess internal
value (and nothing is worth bringing into general cultural
debate, at the level where serious learning is at issue, without
such assessment). So logically my case might make no sense
to a scientist, though I'd like to think otherwise.

The Student Reform Council belongs in Auden's category,
'The fair notion fatally ruined.' There is doubtless a good
argument to be made in favour of a regular channel whereby
undergraduate opinion might be sifted and passed on to the
Colleges and appropriate University bodies. But what is the
obvious prerequisite of success for such a mechanism—
success measured in terms of persuasive power or authority,
or indeed of self-evidently fulfilling a genuine purpose? The
need is clearly to gain the good will and confidence of those
you have to deal with. And your chance of making the sort of
approach calculated to achieve this end will hinge on how
shrewdly and accurately you assess these people.

As it turned out, the SRC's efforts might have been ex-
pressly designed to alienate the senior members and discourage
their participation. There are several conspicuous facts about
dons which might reasonably guide student reformers. Let's
list a few. Teachers in the ancient universities tend to be, in
one way or another, very clever people; they respect, to a
fault, cleverness in others. They usually believe that a university is a place for exceptionally gifted men and women, and
(whilst they differ hugely as to the point at which dilution
sets in) they resent any threat of lower standards of attain-
ment—though it is less the admission than the graduation
stage that most concerns them. They place a high premium

on sheer intelligence and most of them retain, however progressive their political and social beliefs, an old-fashioned notion as to obligations in respect of work (say, during the Long Vacation). Their special baby is a thing called scholarship, of which more in a moment; a concept and an activity they hold to be grossly undervalued in the community at large. They are signalised by good memories, high articulacy, ease and practised poise in abstract debate, attention to detail, verbal exactitude. Often they exhibit a flexibility of viewpoint that baffles and enrages people outside the profession. Rightly or wrongly dons like to believe they are God-given administrative whiz-kids. Sometimes they take more pride in devising a new layout for presenting Kitchen Accounts than in their three-volume history of Byzantine civilisation. But even in this area—what surprises many outsiders—they hold to a correlation between academic and administrative ability in very general terms; especially where academic matters are being administered, for instance in a Tutorial Committee or a Faculty Board. Finally, they are fascinated by themselves and write interminable books and articles on the subject.

Now of course it would be easy to find individual dons to disprove each of these statements in turn. But in general the picture stands; and that makes it all the more extraordinary that student protest of late should have gone out of its way to jump on so many toes. SRC reports seem to be drafted by people who think that the University's destinies are guided by a strange amalgam of people—sometimes pedantic and senile nits, sometimes hustling but moderately successful businessmen, sometimes mindless bureaucrats. To judge by articles in *Varsity* and elsewhere, it would appear that change is blocked in Cambridge by a cabal whose intellectual characteristics are that they are clever-clever, silly or just plain dull. Sexually these people are prudish, prurient or deviant. Personally, the implication goes, they are frightened, malicious, and

visited by the sort of pococurantism which Macaulay attributes to Horace Walpole. Their most cherished beliefs—
illusions—are, of course, quite unexamined. It was characteristic of this frame of mind that Mr Patrick Parrinder, in a
Cambridge Review article on the aims of the SRC, should
refer to the 'pieties' which dons invoke in defending tradi-
tional college loyalties and the like: only dons have pieties,
undergraduates have reasoned convictions. And that he should
hint, too, of a 'conspiracy' by which corrupt senior members
apparently ganged together to thwart progress. This is absurd.
The fact is that academics have many faults, but holding
unconsidered and unchallenged opinions, through mere force
of habit, is just what their job forbids them. They may be
conservative, but that's different.

If reformist circles want their protests to strike home they
ought to consider modifying their approach in a number of
ways. They might spend less time and energy on seeking to
appear good committee-men, to start with. In the nature of
things they aren't going to impress those who've spent a lifetime cultivating this very skill, and who take for granted
anyway the externals of report presentation: the provision
of skimpy tables at the close, for instance. (Most student
reports, in my experience, would benefit from instant appen-
dectomy.) A great many arguments put forward will already
be long familiar to their readers; and the minor presentational
virtues are likely to be far less effective than outright qualities
of brilliance and subtlety in dialectic—qualities which
(if Mr Parrinder will forgive the observation) dons tend to find
rare and welcome in their contact with individual students,
and practically nonexistent in official committee-style reports
—which is one good reason for multiplying the former rather
than the latter. The techniques of midget wrestling are all
very well in their place; but gifted undergraduates have something better to offer. All they need is a decent awareness of
the interests and predispositions of their audience.

Another gratuitous *ad hominem* insult, odd to find in a great university, lies in the depreciation, implicit or explicit, of scholarly work. The special penumbra of moral and intellectual benefit which scholarship brings in its wake is, unfortunately, something you only find out about when you've done some; and you don't have to go very far in the echelons of educational power to find able men and women totally innocent of its existence. I can only repeat here what I wrote some time ago: nothing that has happened since makes me wish to change a word:

'It isn't very widely realised (even, if I may say it without patronage, among undergraduates) how central to a university the presence of gifted scholars is. The virtues of scholarship are quite inseparable from the virtues of a really thriving university: the morale, the sense of purpose, the whole *raison d'être* of the place are intimately connected with this factor. If you don't have men and women teaching who know, in an internal and personal fashion, what academic work is really about, then your teaching will be bad and inappropriate to the setting. . . . And this is true for any university carrying out its day-to-day instruction, not just those after Nobel Prizes and research foundation awards.'

Again, you may not happen to believe that the function of conserving knowledge is quite as important as those of augmenting and communicating knowledge. But most dons believe this, like myself; and reformers ought at least to come to terms with such views, rather than simply ignore them as inconvenient aberrations. That goes, too, for a number of other convictions I'll list briefly, without arguing them out fully. Not too many undergraduates appear to share them: how far this can be said to weaken them I'm not sure.

1. Undergraduates come to Cambridge not for a sort of humanistically conceived self-fulfilment, but to acquire learning—a complicated, tiresome and precarious business. The basic qualification needed is a serious interest in speculative

ideas; the only thing Cambridge is uniquely fitted to do is to
promote a rigorous yet free play of the mind. Anybody who
wants something different should go elsewhere.

2. The most shameful feature of the University today is the
abysmal standard of work on which it's still possible to scrape
a poor Third or a Special. I don't know what to say about the
'Where?' findings on university 'wastage', as reported in the
Observer. Admittedly there's evidence of some capriciousness
in the operation of the guillotine, both within and between
universities. But anybody who doubts that an appreciable
proportion of students (perhaps up to 30 or 35 per cent of
the national intake) could be advantageously dispensed with
must have some pretty lax ideas of what academic training
means, along with a grandly cavalier attitude to the fabric
of university life.

3. Cambridge right now faces a crisis of confidence. It still
has the equipment to bestow on its students, whether they
appreciate it or not, a rare and special kind of education.
Through a combination of past wisdom and mere good for-
tune, we can resist what might be called the Brightonisation
of our universities (I don't think this is an invidious label, for
reasons that will appear in a moment). Many undergraduates
are here more or less by accident; most dons because they
chose to be. We have not normally been thrown out by the
University College of South Wales and Monmouthshire, to
put it crudely; we happen to believe in the college system,
for instance, and we respect the opportunities the place gives
us both as learners and teachers. We aren't unduly worried
when Mr Bernard Crick points out that we have several professors of theology and no professors of sociology—there's no
doubt which the serious student of ideas and cultural development (at a level deeper than the top-third) would rather have
around.

Not all these beliefs are common to dons. But they are
much more widely held amongst senior members than among

student activists, who naturally enough have taken more account of the mod image cultivated by some universities. I'll turn to this issue now.

I said that it didn't seem invidious to associate Sussex with many of the patterns of thinking found in undergraduate argument. In fact I wouldn't gratuitously comment on so recent a foundation, of which moreover so little has been heard scholarship- and research-wise. But it so happens there is a symposium, with the rather grandiloquent title *The Idea of A New University*, which sets out fully and unequivocally the aims of the place. I'm bound to say I find it a revealing document.

One of the key terms in the book is the 'relevance' of courses to students' needs and interests. In one way or another the tactical effect to which this term is put can be seen as covert denigration of serious and disinterested academic study. Nobody will be very surprised or worried that the undergraduate contributor gives evidence of this cast of mind, though it does involve him in laborious silliness : 'One of the most marked effects of the Arts courses at Sussex is that it turns people out into the world around them (universities, of course, are not part of the world, but unidentified extraterrestrial objects); the campus could easily dominate one's entire life, were it not that the type of approach characterized by the Contemporary Britain paper goes a long way towards killing one's apathy and insularity. One is encouraged to think that learning for its own sake, without commitment, is useless. It is very significant that of my own year a large proportion of people wish to work in underdeveloped countries when they graduate.' The last fact will no doubt gladden liberal hearts everywhere : how it's *educationally* significant is less clear. The same writer uses a revealing collocation that neatly catches an attitude which prevails throughout the symposium. He speaks of '. . . better guest speakers, more actors, more administrators, inevitably more bureaucrats, smart people

looking for the gay life, academics, students from abroad.
. . .' The easy way 'academics' slip in speaks volumes. An
academic, you gather, is an exotic figure whose status hovers
between that of a Ghanian basketball star and that of an
itinerant UNESCO fund-raiser: an optional extra whose
presence the University, in a fit of benevolent luxury, kindly
agreed to house. But it's only a more sophisticated version of
the same thing when we read this passage in one of the most
weighty contributions, by Professor Martin Wight, Dean of
the School of European Studies: 'The goal is not to produce
scholars, in the technical sense, but scrupulous and humane
readers, open to a variety of moral and aesthetic experience,
and capable of arriving at true judgment.' What does Professor Wight think scholars are devoting their lives to, if not
this indescribably exacting and indeed painful task of achiev-
ing 'true judgment'—a phrase tossed out with such casual
facility? Once again, the funded experience, the trained intelligence and mass of learning that go to make a fully
educated and humane opinion are set at nothing. A good third-
year man will attain a duly 'open' attitude, and that's that.
Scholars, in the technical or any other sense, are irrelevant.

As indeed they are, in the light of what's confessedly being
attempted at some of the newer foundations. People have
spoken about the Paperback University, but after reading this
symposium I'm inclined to prefer the Digest or the Come As
You Are University. A curriculum of unbelievable modish-
ness is one of the results: 'The fruit of the debate is a highly
selective reading list which extends from *Marx's Economic
and Philosophical Manuscripts of 1844*, and Kierkegaard's
Fear and Trembling, to Rilke, Sartre and Camus and *Dr
Zhivago*. The undergraduate café talk when Mr Betjeman was
at Oxford in the twenties has been distilled into a syllabus.
. . .' Well, you said it. Who needs the Jay twins when
fashionable name-dropping invades the very structure of a
university's intellectual life? Again, Professor Boris Ford

writes with unnecessary hesitance, 'One might say that a
group of social studies defined in this way might be concerned
with the kinds of preoccupation exemplified by Matthew
Arnold and D. H. Lawrence on the one hand, and by Freud,
Durkheim and Riesman on the other, if this collocation can be
allowed to convey a particular flavour of study.' Only too
easily, I'm afraid. This litany of modern culture-heroes belongs
in the chapter on 'Winnie and the Cultural Stream' in *The
Pooh Perplex*, rather than in a serious academic programme.
It has the grisly accuracy of parody.

To the symposium belongs at least the merit of unity.
Exactly the same attitudes are at work in the section by Asa
Briggs. With all deference, I often feel that certain of Professor Briggs' books might have been written by a committee,
and the present chapter gives the impression of emanating
from an academic planning board rather than a single individual deeply engrossed in an area of humane studies. A
representative insistence is on the need 'to incorporate within
the formal university curriculum topics which, although of
great interest to many undergraduates, are usually kept out of
the curriculum and discussed loosely and informally in clubs
and societies'. If you weren't planning a mod university, this
last observation might suggest to you something about the
suitability of such topics for prolonged academic study. (You
aren't, after all, denying the interest of a subject simply by
excluding it from the formal process of teaching and examination.) The same notion of 'relevance' crops up in Professor
David Daiches' contribution, in other respects sanely and
cogently argued : '[The majority of students] come in order
to learn how to come to terms with their own culture and
with their own past, how to clarify their minds, refine their
sensibilities and equip themselves to confront the bewildering
phenomena of modern civilisation. To the pure scholar no
knowledge comes amiss; to most of the young men and
women taking first degrees at a university today the know-

ledge that we offer must not only be meaningful and relevant but must be seen to be so.' I can only say that anybody who approaches classical civilisations, for example, 'in order to learn how to come to terms with their own culture and with their own past' is going to come up with some strange results. Great thinkers have not spent themselves in speculative effort over centuries so that the current generation of teenagers may find their own bearings; and anyone who proceeds on a different assumption risks wild falsification of intellectual history. Incidentally, the very notion of starting a university without a classics department in full working order is misconceived; it will function like *Hamlet* with all the soliloquoys given to Second Gravedigger.

Finally there is a chapter by the senior proctor, Maurice Hutt. Mr Hutt's piece is liberally bestrewn with jargon either offensive or meaningless ('hierarchies and interest-groups', 'peer group acceptance and participation', 'intimate cross-sex relationships'—the best kind too—'group creators and group exercisers' and much more). At times he degenerates into a crazy mixture of socio-metrics, Melanie Klein and the Luce press: 'There are those whose neuroses were, in the closely supervised atmosphere of the school, "success-promoting", but who "decompress" rather unhappily in the less structured atmosphere of the university, getting more alarmed and distressed than is explicable merely by the usual difficulties attendant upon settling in during the first year.' Even if you turn this into English, cutting out some of the straggling participle constructions and giving 'structured' some sort of useful meaning, I don't see how it helps. Mr Hutt makes one or two good observations, as that 'it is probably not immediately apparent to the mass of undergraduates that how they conduct their "private lives" closely affects their acquisition of skills and, still more, their general education'. Yet he can quite happily assert that 'it is still from (the) middle classes that the great majority of undergraduates come', whilst throwing doubt on the idea that 'the norms of English middle class upbringing' can or should be operative in framing disciplinary policy. Mr Hutt has no time at all for the view that the university should act like a reasonably strict parent; it is, apparently, both impracticable and 'quite improper'. There isn't the haziest sense of awareness that a great many parents still send their sons and daughters to university on this very assumption. Mr Hutt blithely assumes it's safely passé, and starts to chat about the declining age of marriage in the country at large.

I've wandered very far off the SRC. But I hope the connection isn't too abstruse. The founding fathers at Sussex evidently hold opinions about many aspects of university life which are commoner among student reformers here than among senior members. Some of my own reasons for holding what are called 'conservative' opinions will, I hope, have emerged. In the rest of the space at my disposal, I will try to draw out certain of these views more explicitly by considering points where I find myself in disagreement with the current student reformist platform.

Firstly. I don't believe 'relevance' is a proper concept to invoke at all in drawing up an academic syllabus. Thomas More is no doubt less relevant than he was a century or two ago; in what way he's become a less appropriate basis of exposition and study I can't imagine. Fifty-seven paperbacks on the crisis in the humanities, with essays by Reinhold Niebuhr and others to solace us in our existential plight, don't supplant a single poem by Milton. The point at issue is whether a given topic is intellectually substantial, taxing and central enough to suit the purposes of the very special sort of mental training which universities exist to provide. The SRC report on teaching mentioned the fact that many undergraduates reading English would have liked to be able to spend more time working on modern American literature. No doubt they find it vivid and personally illuminating; but that doesn't mean it is adapted to the specific needs of academic teaching. I was sorry to see the author of a recent book on Los Angeles, Richard Gilbert (*quem toties amicitiae honorisque nomino*) single out as a noble feature of UCLA the chance it extended to base your Lit. courses on authors like Malamud and Gore Vidal. This betrays the same old therapeutic fallacy: according to which literature is a means of sorting yourself out—to which end, it follows logically enough, a piffling West Coaster is quite as suitable as Samuel Johnson.

Let me come clean: I happen to value most highly a culture which is, to take a few terms at random, civilised, learned, sophisticated, urbane, witty, amused, equable, stratified, devious, ironic, mannered, serene and polite. The Brighton contextual papers seem to consider as uniquely relevant to our times a culture which might be compositely described as angst-ridden, angry, open, explicit, egalitarian, guilt-laden, primitivist, rough in texture, tormented, strident, brutalist and solemn. Everyone who studies the development of ideas will have to make his or her own choice. All I'm concerned to argue is that, leaving aside which is the healthier to inhabit, there's doubt which is a better medium for academic instruction. It's all very well being pastless in a moment of existential dilemma. But culture is of its nature tradition-based, repetitive, working through recurrent myths and publicly sanctified symbols. It has to do with systems of ideas worked out in a commonly agreed framework (I mean ideas-as-embodied-in-living, or in art, not just speculative concepts). Georgian culture is an excellent instance of this happening in depth, though far from the only one of course. It seems to me to offer a more serious educative experience than could ever be derived from a quick pot-holing expedition round the abysses of the Modern European Mind.

Secondly. Take lectures. Sadly, it seems evident that with

many arts subjects lectures are in ribbons. For this I am inclined to blame a habit of mind prevalent among undergraduates and neatly represented by the NUS memorandum to the Hale Committee. There was an instance, too, in the SRC report on teaching, where it was casually mentioned— as though with approval—that many students only went to lectures they found 'stimulating'. Now stimulation is a ridiculously narrow and misleading criterion by which to judge worthwhile undergraduate lectures. The fact is you can't get properly educated without being thoroughly bored for long stretches. Any sound training in the humanities involves a measure of straight informational transmission; and more than that it includes the collocation of many facts in themselves dull or trivial. Not long ago I attended a lecture, not in my own faculty, given by a scholar of justified renown. It was a masterpiece of compression; hundreds of sources had been quietly assimilated and put to use. It was beautifully organised; although there was no showy external 'presentation'— the structure resided in the flow of the ideas themselves. It was shapely and artistic, although quite innocent of TV producer's gimmickry. There was hardly anybody there to hear it, and those who were present put on a show of conspicuous inattention, not to say rudeness. No doubt the SRC jury would have thought this performance uncommercial and voted it down because it didn't stimulate you. Quite so: it did something finer and rarer, it taught you something.

Another point in this connection. It is about time the NUS and similar bodies stopped offering cheap and pharisaic sneers at teachers who find undergraduate instruction distracting and time-consuming amidst their research. Of course it's true that many scholars, who are needless to say the only people competent to teach at true university level, have some difficulty in adjusting themselves to that other part of their work which involves contact with undergraduates. This is not a matter for reproach on the part of those who've never got to the point of finding out what kind of phenomenon research is in the first place. It's an awkward vocational hazard that can only be reduced by care and deep thought on the part of those who have some inkling of how a scholar's mind works. The SRC won't get anywhere if it inherits this silly habit of questioning the presence of learned men within a university; or of trying to force scholars to go round incognito, like a cross between a licensed fool and the disguised king in a folk-tale.

By the way, I note that the Mod Symposium reveals Brighton's disbelief in formal lectures and a policy of cutting their number back severely. If it can be said without malice, this confirms my own faith that they're a good thing and irreplaceable for many purposes. The truth is that lectures are losing ground here (like colleges, vis-à-vis the faculty and department) largely because of a pronounced logrolling operation, set up by people with a variety of motives, ranging from goodish to altogether unworthy, for encouraging their disappearance.

Thirdly, discipline. At the moment we have the comic-pathetic spectacle of young men and women coming up to Cambridge, deeply ignorant of its most serious workings, adolescently contemptuous of its heritage, taking it upon themselves to 'demand' changes (with the reformers' backing) in—let's be blunt—they know not what. If they had any experience of the world they'd realise you can't join great institutions on your own terms: one might add, especially as a junior member—but leave that bit aside. They tout a philosophy of times a-changing which, in its beauty and depth, must derive straight from Bob Dylan. They cling to the sentimental and comforting fallacy that university students aren't and shouldn't be marked off in any way from youth culture at large. They affect to believe that they will emerge intact after three years, and often go a long way to ensure this: another confusion of the social with the educational process. Is it worth repeating that if you do come out 'unscathed', then Cambridge simply hasn't happened as far as you're concerned? In this, old fashioned idealist expectations showed more realism than those current among liberals.

Not so much a summing-up, more a second bite at the cherry. My basic contention is that student reformers should try to come to terms, far more energetically than they have done yet, with the kinds of beliefs and attitudes likely to be found amongst senior members. They should stop kidding themselves that dons oppose proposed change out of automatic conditioning to a few mindless pieties. They should recognise that the inanition and lack of enterprise which clog the Cambridge works often appear on their own side. They should face the fact that they have to deal most commonly with *genuine* intellectuals, as opposed to the watered-down (though equally able) versions who stalk most c's of p. Men and women deeply committed to the life of the mind are perhaps as unfamiliar to a boy or girl coming up as they are to coalheavers, pop singers and actors: unscholarly students often make no serious attempt ever to get on their wavelength. Put more concretely, it's a tactical error to base the style and manner of a report beamed at dons on the productions of a Boilermakers' Society working-party. The logic to convince the Regent House is not necessarily the logic which would sway Westminster, or even Whitehall—though that's a shorter step. In short, reformers ought to find out what the academic life is really about before they start trying to subvert a place which has grown up to promote that life. No matter how good a publicist or a committee-man you become, you won't cut much ice in serious educational discourse (and a small proportion of Cambridge argument really is that), unless you've got some respect for disinterested intellectual activity. Quite simply, the pronouncements of student reformers indicate that they haven't.

The American critic Dwight Macdonald made the observation, a fine and true one, that a people who lose contact with their past become culturally psychotic. In the current neurotic mood of self-laceration, there is a danger Cambridge will suffer a similar fate. We shall reform ourselves out of our own most serious purposes.

Summer 1965

Sentence

JIM PHILIP

a bed of special care
    for sparing
        with his words
        is giant Love,
    yet here we lie
the coupled
        adjectives
        around his nouns
of silence
        as he speaks.

13 February 1965

Dream in the Afternoon

THOMAS WEISKEL

I had barely time to compose my unconcern,
You rammed so playfully into my arms;
Except in this dream, you never learned
Your steps in the dance of my charms.
We were alone : a logging road,
Frozen and drifted into rose shadows
And orange bands where the low sun
Stabbed through the trees; the snow
Sunk our past, changing it to the dream.
Rocked back in your charge, I spluttered, then smiled,
Leaving reality to its own wild
Quarrel with what seemed so real.
Mad and lustless as a brother
You clung and we rolled in a ditch and a peal
Of your ecstasy ricocheted through the orange
Iced woods, and your coat came undone
And helpless my hand began what we feared.
But all that was gone, the old aching,
And your consent was new and soft
And your shiver rose not from the ice, but broke
From deep tear-guarded woods
And bloomed in the last orange rays,
Your gray sighs melted in the snow,
Eroding my sleep, and what I'd hoped would grow.

14 February 1966